Super-Size Your Sales

HOW TO BECOME A SUPER SUCCESSFUL SALESPERSON

Robert L. Bailey

the Peppertree Press
Sarasota, Florida

www.bobbaileyspeaker.com

Copyright © Robert L. Bailey, 2010

All rights reserved. Published by *the* Peppertree Press, LLC.
the Peppertree Press and associated logos are trademarks of
the Peppertree Press, LLC.

No part of this publication may be reproduced, stored in a
retrieval system, transmitted in any form or by any means,
electronic, mechanical, photocopying, recording, or otherwise,
without prior written permission
of the publisher and author/illustrator.
Graphic design by Rebecca Barbier

For information regarding permission,
call 941-922-2662 or contact us at our website:
www.peppertreepublishing.com or write to:
the Peppertree Press, LLC.
Attention: Publisher
1269 First Street, Suite 7
Sarasota, Florida 34236

ISBN: 978-1-936051-98-4

Library of Congress Number: 2010924954

Printed in the U.S.A.

Printed April, 2010

DEDICATION

To the outstanding independent insurance agents who represented my former company. By working with them and observing them, I learned many of the techniques that permitted some salespeople to achieve great success.

And to Sylvia, who tells her friends that her husband's books are "his golf," and to Janet, Nancy, Jim, Jay, Haley, Jenny, Justin, Megan, Zack, Cody, Carson, and the newest members of our family, Jason and Mary Hannah. I'm proud of all of you.

ACKNOWLEDGMENTS

Many people contributed to this book in some way, but the following deserve special note:

Lane Gutstein – This is my third book she has edited very competently. She assumes the job enthusiastically, despite my efforts to make her job difficult. While she is editing the latest version of the manuscript, I'm making further changes, which makes her job nearly impossible. She accepts the challenge gracefully. The errors that remain are my own.

Julie Ann Howell and **Teri Franco**, of Peppertree Press, and graphic designer, **Rebecca Barbier** – I have fun writing books, but getting one published is not fun for me. Julie Ann, Teri and Becky take the pain out of it. They are a delight to work with.

Ken Fields and **Diane Masterson** - Ken is Assistant Vice President and Manager of Sales Development, and Diane is Pacesetter Regional Sales Manager, for the State Auto Insurance Companies. These folks have trained and coached hundreds of successful salespeople. When it comes to sales experts, these two individuals top the list. I appreciate their suggestions for improving this book.

Joe Farr – Joe is now retired, but he has had more sales experience in one lifetime than a half dozen average salespeople. His suggestions were very helpful.

There are so many others who deserve my thanks and appreciation, but any list I might compile would fall short. My sincere thanks to all of you.

CONTENTS

DEDICATION iii
ACKNOWLEDGMENTS v
FOREWORD 1
1 — BUILDING A FOUNDATION 5
2 — PROBLEMS AND GOOD FEELINGS 14
3 — A PLAN TO WIN 21
4 — NO, NO, NO, NO, NO 31
5 — CUSTOMERS ASK ABOUT PRICE
      BUT BUY VALUE..35
6 — TELL TWO PEOPLE 46
7 — LISTEN 54
8 — WHY SHOULD I BUY FROM YOU? 57
9 — PERFECT EQUALITY 63
10 — PACKAGING 69
11 — DOES ANYBODY CARE? 73
12 — LEAVE A MESSAGE AT THE TONE 80
13 — THE ELECTRONIC YELLOW PAGES 84
14 — ASK 90
15 — PROGRAMMED TO WIN 92
   OTHER BOOKS BY ROBERT L. BAILEY 105
   THE AUTHOR 107

FOREWORD

Every, yes every, successful venture requires an effective sales effort. The world's economy is based on sales, not on government spending programs.

You've heard it said nothing happens until somebody sells something. That's an under-statement. The sales process is the bedrock of the free enterprise system.

Too often sales people do not get proper credit. Some believe the word "sales" in a title refers to individuals who are slick, obnoxious and integrity-challenged. Movies and TV generally depict the sales person as a greedy, deceptive, distrustful and selfish person. One company changed the name of its sales people to Business Development Specialists. This is fine, I suppose, but let me assure you there is nothing undignified about sales. It's an honorable profession and one upon which the American economy depends. *It's a business of one professional—a sales person—whose job is helping a buyer make a decision in the buyer's best interest,* just like a doctor or an emergency medical technician.

I've been associated with the property and casualty insurance industry since 1958. Therefore, what I know about the business world and about sales comes from the perspective of an insurance guy.

Yet, I've found the lessons I've learned in the insurance business apply to most fields of business and, in fact, to most non-business fields as well.

Through the years I've worked with thousands of property and casualty insurance agents. Some are absolutely outstanding—exceptionally good and overwhelmingly successful. A few are not so good, and most are somewhere in the middle.

Then a number of years ago I started to study these agents in more depth. Why are some highly successful? Why are others only mediocre performers? Why do some achieve astonishing success while a significant number fails? I found there are certain qualities that separate highly successful salespeople from the crowd. A relatively few, about 4% of the total, have learned the formula for Super-Sizing their sales results. These relatively few often achieved astounding sales success over several years of hard work, involving many mistakes in the process and learning from those mistakes.

From this insurance perspective, I started to observe the sales process in other fields: the automobile salesperson, the real estate agent, the farm implement dealer, the plumber, the building contractor, and even the sales clerk at K-Mart or Walmart, or the checker at the supermarket or the clerk at the dry cleaners. I noted, without question, the sales characteristics that make certain insurance agents highly successful are the same characteristics that bring about success in other ventures. The characteristics that permit great salespeople to Super-Size their sales have been captured in this book.

Success in sales, or in any other field, is not an accident, nor is it a product of being smart enough to select the right parents. Perhaps luck or inheritance can have a short-term effect on success, but you've probably noted that many people "born with a silver spoon in their mouths" soon run through the family fortune or are otherwise unable to build upon the advantage they inherited.

Super-Sizing sales over the long term is nearly always the result of the application of certain success principles that only a relatively few have learned to apply consistently. That's why great CEO's are usually great salespeople, and why some 85% of CEO's come from a sales background. Great CEO's tend to be great communicators, and great salespeople also tend to be great communicators.

By choosing to read this book and applying the sales principles you will learn here, you're well on your way to Super-Sizing your sales. You can become one of America's most successful salespeople, and you'll be able to perpetuate your success throughout your career.

This process is not rocket science. As you read *Super-Size Your Sales,* you'll note the skills required for achieving superior sales success are readily available to you. It's more a product of desire and commitment than genius. And you will find your pursuit of sales success is fun and personally rewarding.

Are you ready to achieve remarkable sales success only a comparatively few enjoy?

Let's get started! *Super-Size Your Sales!*

BUILDING A FOUNDATION

During the past 40 years we have always purchased American-made cars. I make American money, so I believed we had an obligation to buy American-made cars.

But the service at our dealership continued to erode. My older and less nimble 6 foot 4 inch frame had greater difficulty getting in and out of smaller and smaller Cadillacs, and we had some concern about the financial condition of General Motors; therefore, we decided to look elsewhere.

After recommendation by a friend, a BMW dealership was our first stop, and here we ran into what had to be the world's worst car salesman. He didn't ask our names, and he didn't give us his name, but he did show us some nice but expensive cars. When we expressed interest in one model, he never suggested we go for a demonstration drive. Instead, he pointed to the sticker on the rear window and said, "This is what it costs. Take it or leave it. If you don't want to buy it, that's okay with me. Somebody else will."

"I don't want to deprive another customer of the opportunity to buy this car," I answered. My wife Sylvia and I left the dealership, drove a few blocks down the street, bought a new Lexus within the hour and paid cash for it.

Sales careers generally don't last long if they're not built on solid foundations, and this salesman didn't put the first building block into place.

There's nothing particularly glamorous about building a foundation. It's generally not especially attractive; it seldom involves sophisticated technology; its very existence may not be obvious. When buying a building, few even ask about the type of foundation on which it is built. Yet it is probably the most important element in having assurance a building will stand the test of time. You can be sure a building won't last long if it's not built on a solid foundation.

A proper foundation is the critical first step in Super-Sizing your sales, helping you reach the top and stay at the top throughout your sales career.

Several years ago we were building a new home in the Columbus, Ohio area. Our builder sent us to a wholesale place to select floor coverings. The sales people kept referring to us as Lot 15. "This hardwood flooring will look great in your entryway, Lot 15. Lot 15, this ceramic tile will be perfect for your master bath."

Time passed and I had forgotten about the Lot 15 people until one day when there was a tie-up on Interstate 71. I took the first exit and drove through a part of the city I didn't normally visit, right by the builders' supply company. Waist-high weeds had grown up in the parking lot, and a huge For Sale or Lease sign was posted in front of the building.

I can't be certain failing to call customers by name brought about the company's demise, but I can say with certainty its odds for survival would have been greater had they treated customers differently.

The American people are screaming for simple courtesy, personal attention, fast service, and ongoing personal relationships. And when they get it, buyers put a handsome price tag on it.

Yet simple courtesy and personal attention occur in a relatively small percentage of sales transactions. Not long ago I needed to repair a piece of pool equipment. I arrived at the store at about 8:50 a.m., found a parking place directly in front of the store, and decided to wait until the store opened at 9. A few minutes after nine, the manager unlocked the door as I waited outside. I opened the door, and he turned to walk away. I was perhaps ten paces behind as I followed him into the store, found the item I needed, and proceeded to the cash register to pay. Not once did he speak or acknowledge in any way a real live paying customer was present, even though I was the only customer in the store at the time. If there is any other purchasing alternative when I need another product of this type, I will purchase it elsewhere.

Similar experiences occur every day. Sylvia and I found the item we needed at a "big box" store and got in the check-out line to pay. I noticed the cashier never said one word to customers in front of us. "I'm going to get him to talk to us," I told Sylvia. When we arrived at the register, I said with great enthusiasm, "Good morning." The cashier didn't respond. "How are you doing today?" Again he said nothing. "Isn't this a beautiful day?" No response. "Are you folks going to make it?" I asked, referring to the store's bankruptcy status. "I want you to succeed. I don't want folks like you to lose their jobs," I continued, never with one word of acknowledgment.

While many factors played a role in the store's lack of success, it isn't a huge surprise the company has struggled to survive.

Perhaps there are a few products or services inherently fun to buy. But for people like me, buying most products or services is a most detested activity. Shopping is not among my one thousand highest priorities. I would rather be someplace else; therefore, it's your job as a professional salesperson to turn the sales process into a pleasant, almost fun, experience. No hassle, no high pressure, and pleasant!

Your customer or prospect, the one standing before you this very moment, may be worth millions of dollars of income to you. If you doubt that statement, I'll provide compelling proof later in this book. How you treat this customer or potential customer is the foundation upon which a successful sales career is built. These simple characteristics add value to the sales process, a form of value relatively uncommon in most American sales transactions:

Begin with a cheery "good morning" and shake hands. Introduce yourself if the friendship was not already established. Treat the customer like a good friend, as if he or she is a guest in your home. Be the real you, not a phony you with an air of superiority that turns people off. The words you use should be your own, words that reflect your own personality, not something you've memorized from a sales book.

It's hard to put a dollar sign on a greeting, but nevertheless it's value. Compare this enthusiastic greeting to the salesperson who never bothers to smile and speak or carries on a conversation with an associate without missing a syllable, never with an acknowledgment that a customer is near. I know you've had experiences like this, and it's likely you become as irritated with this behavior as I do. Even a smile and a *good afternoon, sir*, would have added value to the transaction.

Listen. If you don't understand the name, ask again, even if you have to ask the customer to spell it for you. People don't mind (and in fact are impressed) that you care enough to learn their names. As soon as you're alone, write it down on a four by six inch card, along with any personal information disclosed during the visit.

For more than 30 years we bought a new Cadillac every two years. We made this known during our visits with sales people. You would think this personal information might have been noted by the salesperson and I would receive a call perhaps 22 or 23 months later suggesting we try out a new model. Not once have we received such a call. There's a gold mine within the personal information shared during the sales process.

Look your customer in the eye, giving your undivided attention as if this person were the most important person in the world. Use your customer's name often, the sweetest sounding words in the entire English language.

No one can quarrel with the success of Walmart. Sam Walton insisted on his ten-foot rule. When a Walmart associate is within ten feet of a customer, he or she is expected to smile and speak to the customer. That's value, a practice largely ignored today.

Kroger Food Stores have taken it another step with its 7/7 rule: eye contact within seven seconds, smile and speak within seven feet of the customer. It's a great idea, one management should be emphasizing to all employees.

You are friendly and you extend the same courtesies you would extend to guests in your home. It is obvious you really care about your customer.

You have a pleasant smile and are enjoyable to be

around. Your smile is contagious. Your mannerisms are upbeat. It will be evident you truly like your job. I can recall hundreds of sales transactions in which the salesperson gave me the impression he or she hated the job. Some go so far to say, "Tomorrow is going to be better because I have the day off."

You appear to like—no, you *really* like—your customer. Your mannerisms make it clear you enjoy working with your customer. What a contrast to many shopping experiences when salespeople give the impression, "This job would be okay if it weren't for people like you who come in here and bother me."

You do what you say you will do when you say you will do it. You are willing to go the extra mile to assure customer satisfaction. If a return phone call is promised by 3 p.m., the call is returned by 3 p.m. Death is no excuse. You promise to be there between 9 and 10 a.m. on Wednesday; you're there on time as promised.

It's almost epidemic for sales and service people not to show up at the appointed time. When tardiness occurs, it's a black mark on you and your company. If you're five minutes late, call. And when you arrive, apologize. Your client's time is worth as much as yours.

You exude confidence and trust, giving your customer greater confidence the purchasing decision was the right choice. Trust is essential if you are to build customer loyalty. The customer expects total integrity.

"But I'm not a morning person," some say. Or, "I'm not a people person." Well, learn the skills. New habits can generally be established in about 30 days. If you haven't smiled for awhile, try it again. It doesn't hurt; I promise. Try an enthusiastic "good morning" or "good afternoon" with a smile. Look your customer in the eye and act like you mean it.

Building a Foundation

Once a business relationship has been established, great salespeople expand their knowledge base. They learn the name of the customer's spouse, the names of the kids, where they're going to school, the family's hobbies, perhaps even the name of the dog. Add this information to your four by six file card. Universally we humans are interested in one thing more than anything else in the world—ourselves and our families.

One marketing guru says building a solid customer relationship is like asking for a date. Don't ask to get married on the first date. Don't talk about yourself. Get to know the customer and his or her needs. It takes time to build a long-term business relationship.

Consistently America's most successful salespeople display these characteristics. One very successful insurance agent, in addition to smiling and speaking to everyone, never lets a piece of correspondence go out of his office, even those prepared by computer, unless it contains a short hand-written note pertaining specifically to the individual receiving the mailing: "Congratulations on receiving the Rotary Club award. It was well deserved." "Sorry to hear Judy is under the weather. Hope she is feeling better soon." "How does Bill like college? He's a smart young man and I know he will do well." Every client, every prospect, every person with whom he has contact senses his friendly nature and knows he has a personal, non-selfish interest in them and their families.

Another very successful agent presents the same friendly approach to those around him and insists every staff member do the same. "We hire only people who are inherently friendly, people who like people," he says. "We like the cheerleader type. We think it's easier to teach new employees the technical part of our business than it is to teach them the people skills our customers have come to expect from us."

Over the next several months, analyze and categorize your own purchasing decisions. Why did you buy certain products and services? Why did you choose to do business with certain firms and salespeople? What drove your buying decisions? Such an analysis will help you understand how relationships with people control most buying decisions.

Nearly 20 years ago I asked the presidents of two major bank holding companies the same question, "What do you think your bank will look like in ten years?"

Surprisingly, I got similar answers from both. They wanted to sell their branch banks and lease them back for ten years, for in ten years they would not have a branch bank network. The branches were expensive real estate and required extensive human resources, resources they would not need with the emerging technology. To encourage customers to use automated teller services, some banks were requiring customers to pay for teller services. They wanted customers to use ATM machines, not expensive people.

If a customer needed money to buy a new car or refrigerator, they wanted him or her to draw on a line of credit. If a customer needed serious money for a business, they wanted the customer to drive downtown to the main bank and talk to a loan officer. But whatever you do, don't use the branch banks and don't talk to our people—it's too expensive.

In looking back, the bank CEOs were off target. The American people rebelled to pay-for-teller service. They wanted conveniently located branch banks with personal contact and personal relationships with people. Today there are more branch banks than ever.

Whatever you buy—from a new suit to a pair of socks, from an insurance policy to cell phone service—the courtesy and friendliness of the salesperson play a significant role in the decision process. This is the foundation that enables you to *Super-Size Your Sales.*

Indifference is the reason most customers choose not to return to a place of business. And when a customer experiences rudeness on the part of the salesperson, 60% will go elsewhere, even though it's more inconvenient and the prices are higher.

Certainly other factors which we will discuss later bear on the sales process. But most sales transactions are sealed when the salesperson adds the value of courtesy, friendliness and a caring attitude, characteristics too often ignored in American business today.

Simple stuff—skills most people possess already. McDonalds taught Americans to bus their own tables; therefore, it shouldn't be expecting too much for salespeople to learn to make eye contact with the customer, smile, say "good morning" or "good afternoon," and "thank you" for making the purchase or for stopping by.

This is the foundation of success in sales. This is the critical prerequisite to enable you *to Super-Size Your Sales.* Without common courtesy (which is relatively uncommon in business today), friendliness and a caring attitude, a long-term business relationship will not develop. The most critical characteristics of all sales transactions are the "good feelings" you generate during the sales process.

Earlier in this chapter I told you this one customer may be worth millions of dollars of income to you. Well, let's say he or she makes a purchase of a modest amount, or perhaps leaves without making a purchase at all. Where do the multi-millions come in?

Because of your courtesy, friendliness, caring attitude and the "good feelings" of dealing with you, I can assure you the pay-back will be substantial. Stick with me.

PROBLEMS AND GOOD FEELINGS

Great salespeople are in the business of solving problems. The customer has a problem or a need. You, the salesperson, must become an assistant buyer. You must solve the problem or fill the need from the perspective of the customer. But there's more to it than simply solving problems.

Every purchase involves one of two things, either a solution to a problem or good feelings. Think about it with regard to your own purchasing decisions.

Let's say you take your spouse out to eat. Does this involve a solution to a problem or good feelings? Certainly you need to solve a problem. You and your spouse need nourishment. But the need for nourishment can be solved for $3 by ordering from the Super Value menu at Wendy's or McDonald's or from the sandwich machine at the local gasoline station.

Most dining experiences, however, go well beyond

Problems And Good Feelings

the need for nourishment and encompass good feelings as well. A meal out with candlelight, wine, white glove service, and a check for $80 per person likewise solves the problem of needing nourishment, but the most significant portion of the check is for good feelings.

The difference between a $3.00 meal and an $80 meal is $77. Diners are therefore paying $3 for nourishment and perhaps $77 for ambiance, good service, wine and candle light—or good feelings.

Every day thousands of new cars are sold. Most buyers will say they bought the car because they need dependable transportation. Yet a $6,000 used Chevy with 50,000 miles on it will likely get you to and from work, will transport the kids to school, and will get you to the grocery store and back. The difference between a $6,000 used car, which solves the problem, and, say, a $70,000 Mercedes is $64,000—the amount the buyer is paying for good feelings—prestige, comfort, fancy leather seats, the surround-sound speaker system, a GPS system that tells you how to get to and from the supermarket, and a whiff of the delightful new-car smell. Ah—the joy and good feelings associated with ownership of a fancy new car!

Obviously property values fluctuate widely between small towns and larger cities, as well as in different parts of the country. Let's say in your community a reasonably comfortable house can be purchased for $150,000, but there are probably homes on the market for $1 million or more. Both homes provide adequate shelter, the solution to the buyer's problem. The difference between $150,000 and $1 million is $850,000, the amount the home buyer is paying for the good feelings of status, prestige, comfort and convenience.

So it goes with most purchases. Most products and services involve a combination of good feelings and solutions to problems, with the greater portion of the dollar going for good feelings. It's seldom a price issue. It's generally a value issue, and good feelings translate to value. I have yet to meet a person whose goal in life is to wear the cheapest clothes, eat the cheapest food, drive the cheapest car, or live in the cheapest house.

Prospects and customers must first be satisfied with the "good feelings" dimension of the product, service and the sales process. Without the good feelings, you will likely not have an opportunity to solve customers' problems. Having cleared the good feelings hurdle, professional salespeople are now ready to solve customers' problems. When customers make an appointment with you, they do so for one reason: you offer a product or service they need to solve a problem.

To solve the problem, you must know your business thoroughly—upside down and backward. This is a prerequisite of success. There is no shortcut. Without exception, top salespeople are experts in the products or services they sell. You must be an expert in your field.

In the real estate field, this means knowing the market; knowing values; knowing zoning; and understanding property tax trends. What are the chances someone will build a drive-in restaurant next door? Is a new freeway planned in the adjoining block?

Is the property being considered a part of a Community Development District which may impose taxes and fees for managing and financing infrastructure? If there are community assessments, have reserves been established to pay for infrastructure needs? Are assessments and dues increasing each year? What are plans for the future? How many homes in the community or units of a condominium are owned by investors? How many units are in foreclosure or bankruptcy, placing a greater financial burden on active owners? As an "assistant buyer," you must be able to advise your customer. While sharing the facts with the customer may cost this particular sale, *not* sharing the facts may cost many future sales.

Perhaps you're willing to pay a premium for a home backing onto a beautiful golf course, but who controls the golf course? Once all lots are sold, will the developer close the golf course and build homes on it? This happens often.

Where are the schools and bus stops? How convenient is shopping? Friends bought a beautiful home but learned later it is a 30 minute drive to the supermarket.

Under what building code was the home built? In Florida, where I live, homes built under the most recent building code are much less likely to be blown away in a hurricane. Does the home contain Chinese drywall or other forms of toxic drywall which is causing a huge problem today?

Sylvia and I have owned ten homes during our married life, as well as a number of investment properties, so we have dealt with a good number of real estate salespeople. On two or three occasions when a realtor called for an appointment to show our home, we said, "We can't leave right now. We're expecting an important phone call" or some other reason. "Can you show the house at a different time so we can leave during the showing?" The realtor has said, "It's okay if you're there." So on a few occasions we have seen realtors in action.

And here's what we saw: "This is the kitchen; this is the family room; this is the bathroom." Very perceptive. They looked down at the potty and knew immediately this was the bathroom.

Obviously, this showing wasn't very professional. At no time did the realtor explain features of the home, either positive or negative.

We've asked a couple of friends if they had ever been home when their house was shown, and they saw similar behavior: This is the kitchen and this is the bathroom.

Know your business. Know the features of the property being sold. And know the upside and downside of this particular property or location.

In the property and casualty insurance field, in which I spent my "first life," I can list hundreds of examples in which the buyer was well served. Exposures to loss were properly evaluated and appropriate insurance coverage or risk management measures were recommended. I can also list hundreds of disasters in which exposures were not properly evaluated and proper insurance coverage was not placed in effect. Some agents were experts in their field; others were not.

And so it goes in any field. What's the difference between Product A and Product B? They may look the same to the buyer. Do the differences justify a higher price? On dozens of occasions I've asked sales people to explain the differences between Product A and B. If the sales person is able to point out differences and values, I generally buy the best and most expensive product.

I've known salespeople who are absolute authorities in product knowledge, but they haven't been successful as salespeople because they try to dazzle the customer with their broad knowledge; consequently they leave the customer bewildered, confused and unwilling to buy. Great salespeople must use their vast knowledge selectively to answer specific questions or solve individual problems.

A few days ago we were looking for a product which appeared to be what we wanted, but the salesperson talked, and talked, and talked—about his aunt who had a stroke, about his wife's job, about his home, about his addiction

Problems And Good Feelings

to cigarettes—turning the sales presentation into an hour and a half ordeal. It was all about me, me, me, the salesperson, not you, you, you the customer. We intend to buy elsewhere.

Very successful salespeople also sell great products and great services—no junk and no shoddy stuff. The salesperson's name is indelibly stamped on every product or service delivered to the customer. A tainted product or one with marginal value casts the salesperson in the same light.

This is not to say top-level salespeople sell only higher quality products and services. Offering an array of products from the very highest quality to the mediocre often helps the salesperson meet the needs of the customer who has been shopping. "We have a similar product available," the salesperson explains, "but it's not one we can recommend to our customers, and here's why."

Successful salespeople have tremendous enthusiasm for the products or services they sell. They believe in them. They personally buy these products or services for themselves and their families and are confident they would not violate friendships by recommending these products or services to their closest friends.

The last four letters of the word *enthusiasm*—IASM—mean *I Am Sold Myself*. Top salespeople love the business, are enthusiastic about serving customers, and are believers. It doesn't take long for this enthusiasm to show through. Great salespeople are genuine through and through and would never mislead or lie, whether or not an immediate sale depends upon a slight deception. They're always going to do their level best to give great value and overwhelming service to customers and solve their problems in the most appropriate manner. Providing commodity products or services (doing just what everybody else is doing) usually doesn't separate the salesperson from the pack. Great expertise is an essential quality.

Great salespeople have learned to solve customers' problems with extraordinary product knowledge. This requires thorough knowledge of their products and services as well as knowledge of new products and industry developments through continuing education. Products change and needs change. It's essential you continue to learn throughout your career.

Sales are made under a canopy of trust and credibility, and trust and credibility can be easily fractured when the salesperson has less than thorough expertise in the field.

Do you remember the birth and death dates of George Washington? Abraham Lincoln? Martin Luther King? Few know these dates, yet these dates appear on the tomb stones of famous people as well as the rest of us, with a dash between the dates. In *Presentations* magazine, Dr. Vincent Muli Kituku, says, "Yet the dash is the most important thing. We remember the dash in between the dates, but we don't remember the dates."

The dash between the date of your birth and the date you die represents what people will remember about you, and the dash is strongly influenced by your ability to solve your customers' problems with thorough product knowledge wrapped in a generous supply of good feelings.

A PLAN TO WIN

Sales plans are all over the lot. Some are good; some are not so good; some are written down; others are not. Many underperformers don't have sales plans or goals at all. They spend more time planning a five-day vacation than they do planning their careers.

I recommend you write down specific sales goals. Carry the list with you. Review your goals every day. You must have goals. You must have a plan to win.

There's a classic story of a Fuller Brush salesman who was a top producer in the United States year after year. A regional sales manager of a life insurance company heard about this salesman's success and imagined just how effective he would be as a life insurance salesman. The sales manager looked him up and found he was an immigrant who spoke broken English and who had little formal education.

The sales manager impressed the brush salesman with the amount of money he could make as a life insurance salesman, and he was persuaded to take a battery of aptitude tests.

He failed the tests in virtually every regard. The tests showed he knew little about life insurance, had little interest in learning, and generally didn't have great respect for life insurance people. Selling life insurance was about the last thing on earth he wanted to do.

The sales manager was ready to write him off as a bad idea and was bidding the brush salesman goodbye when the president of the company happened along. The president was told of this man's outstanding success as a Fuller Brush salesman as well as his poor performance on the aptitude tests.

"About how many people do you see a day when selling Fuller Brushes?" the president asked.

"Well, I try to see 20 people a day," the brush salesman answered.

"Hire him," the president ordered. "He doesn't need an aptitude."

And indeed he didn't need an aptitude. He became the company's leading life insurance salesperson year after year.

This man had a plan—not a sophisticated plan, but a plan—a plan to see 20 people a day.

I can't imagine anyone keeping such a pace year after year. And it may not be possible with certain products or services, but this is the kind of plan it takes to be overwhelmingly successful.

Most successful sales people are successful because they work at it. They don't take Monday off because Monday is a bad day. They don't take Friday off because they're trying to slow down for the weekend. They work at it day after day.

A few years ago Sylvia and I were shopping for a new

car. We returned to the dealership and were waiting for the salesman with whom we had dealt a few days earlier when we noted sales award plaques on the wall. One person's name was shown as the top salesperson this year, and last year, and the year before. Looking around the showroom, we noticed the salesperson was at his desk on the perimeter of the showroom and was not busy at the moment. I approached him, congratulated him on his outstanding sales record, and asked, "How do you do it? How are you able to be the top salesperson in this agency year after year?"

"It's easy," he responded. "I'm here."

He explained selling cars is his job, and he shows up for work every day, just as any person who has a full-time job. He doesn't take time off just because he doesn't feel like working. He doesn't take time off to run personal errands. He's there—on the job. His plan was to be there six days a week.

If you've watched the professional golfers at a PGA tournament, it's easy to see why they're successful. They work at it. The top golfers are hitting balls on the driving range and putting on the practice green before their rounds. Then they play 18 holes of competitive golf. Following this grueling competition, they're back on the driving range and the practice green. This is the routine day after day. They do what most of us don't want to do; they work at it hours on end.

They are bound to get tired of this demanding routine once in awhile, but the activity is bearable because their eyes are on the goal. There are only 2.5 strokes difference between the golfer at the top of the money list and the 126th player on the money list.

I was raised on a farm in Kansas and once owned a farm in Ohio. If my goal was to increase my income from soybeans by 20% next year, I could approach it in several ways. First, I could hope the price of soybeans is 20% higher next year, or I could hope for a blockbuster yield and produce 20% more soybeans per acre. But chances are neither of these circumstances will come about.

The greatest likelihood of increasing my income from soybeans by 20% next year is to plant 20% more acres to soybeans. In other words, *my goal should be activity based and not results based.* Positive results can occur only if the activities producing those results have increased.

Larry Wilson is a world-renowned entrepreneur, speaker and facilitator who had great success as a life insurance salesman. Early in his career he was miserable, failing and planning to get out of the sales field. Fortunately, an exceptional manager helped him rethink and reframe his negative experiences as a salesman.

Larry's manager pointed out, like most rookies, he had to call on about 20 prospects to make one sale. And the average commission on the policy he was selling was about $500. Therefore, after each sales call, he said to himself, "Thanks for the $25."

Over time, as his skills improved and confidence increased, the average commission increased and the number of calls required for a sale decreased. Soon he was able to say to himself following a call, "Thanks for the $100." This process helped Larry build a tolerance for rejection. The story is told in his excellent book, *Play to Win* (Bard Press).

Throughout my business career I reviewed and rewrote my goals at the beginning of each new year. I carried those goals with me at all times and re-read them every morning. My goals were divided into three categories; business, personal, and family.

Each of us is inherently drawn closer to the things we consistently think about. Therefore, if we write down our goals and concentrate on them every day, we are moved gradually toward doing the things we have to do to achieve those goals. I didn't always achieve every goal on my list, but I believe it's safe to say I came much closer to achieving them than if they had not been written down and reviewed daily.

Analyze the results of your sales efforts. Which type of customer produced the most profitable results? Which type of sales activity produced the best result? Based on these answers, how many additional activities do you need to perform if you are to increase your sales by 10%, 20%, 30% or more?

One very successful insurance agency gave credit for its outstanding success to a simple concept of writing five sales letters a day to prospects—not emails, not typewritten, but hand written, with licked postage stamps. They found 84% of its new business came from these five letters.

Successful retail stores have used technology to understand their customers and their buying habits. This technology to a degree accounts for the success of Walmart while K-Mart struggled. Walmart knows whether blue sweaters are selling better than red sweaters and stocks its shelves accordingly. Walmart knows what's in stock; K-Mart often does not.

At one of our agents' meetings, I visited with an agent who had spent an inordinate amount of time trying to find an insurance market for a fleet of fishing boats. He represented no insurance company that specialized in that market. He had no expertise in this market.

I asked, "Would it be to your client's advantage, and to your advantage, if you simply referred this client to an agent and an insurer that specializes in fishing boats?"

The agent answered, "Oh no! Just look at the commission I can make on this account."

If the agent would have analyzed the time he spent on this potential account, he would have found he could have made a lot more income by concentrating on those markets he had the expertise to serve.

In far too many cases sales people don't prospect for customers with the greatest sales and profit potential. This is not to say sales people should be rude to any prospect or customer. Every individual has certain circles of friends and associates, some of whom will be in the salesperson's target market. No individual should be offended.

When reviewing the activities, you may find certain activities do not contribute to sales. Can these activities be eliminated or reduced? For instance, how many unneeded committee meetings are you attending each week?

I'm often accused of being anti-golf, but it's not the case. I'm only opposed to calling golf a business activity if it does not contribute to your business objectives. One insurance agent told me how important golf is to his success. He said he sells a lot of insurance because of his golf course connections.

"Can you name for me one account you have picked up over the last three months because of golf?" I asked. He stammered for a couple of minutes and admitted he probably hadn't sold any insurance. So his thrice-weekly golf outings with the same three guys, with an investment of probably more than 15 hours a week, had to be chalked up as a social activity, not a business activity.

Too often business goals are akin to New Year's resolutions. They are soon forgotten. Fitness centers find their busiest month of the year is January with many new customers who have made resolutions to get fit. By the first of February business activity is back to normal.

It takes commitment to stay on course. Although I condemn needless committee meetings that accomplish little, I do recommend a mastermind group that pulls you up when you get discouraged. The group should be small, not more than three or four members, and they have to be positive people who encourage you, not pull you down. This means it's not easy to put such a group together. Too many people see the glass as half empty rather than half full. Meetings should be short, maybe 15 to 30 minutes over early-morning coffee once a month.

America's most successful salespeople listen to their customers. They send thank you notes. They answer email personally. They do everything possible to build excellent customer relationships. They set high goals and they pursue those goals with passion.

Top salespeople know what they want in life, and they go after it. Nothing can dilute their efforts or take them off course. Focus—don't scattergun your efforts. Intensity of purpose nearly always produces success.

One sales manager challenged his people, "How successful would you be if you knew you would die if you failed to achieve your goal?" Most agreed they could reach it if they knew there was such a penalty. At the same time, they maintain balance in their lives—a balance of family, God, and other worthy outside activities.

Outstanding sales people have chosen to succeed. It's not a matter of genius; it's not a matter of luck; it's not a matter of being assigned a good territory; it's not a matter of inheriting a special success gene. They have a burning desire to win. They have simply decided they will be successful. This decision and the resultant attitude produce a chain of events which bring success. Therefore, success is a matter of choice.

Dr. Karl Menninger, a famous psychiatrist, was asked

to give the secret of good mental health. He said, "Find a mission and pursue it intensely." That's true for mental health; it's true for physical health too.

Those of us who are less successful, on the other hand, can't quite decide what we want in life. We jump from mission to mission while trying to decide what we want to do "when we grow up." We may decide one goal is not attainable, so we move in another direction on a whim.

I know a man who is a nice guy and very capable. He retired not long ago without having accomplished a great deal in life because he couldn't stick to one goal long enough to achieve it. He jumped from job to job because "this is an opportunity of a lifetime." He sometimes called these new options "golden rings." He said, "You've got to grab the golden ring when it swings by." Soon after grabbing "a golden ring," he found this new "opportunity of a lifetime" presented no more potential, and perhaps less potential, than the job he just left.

America's top salespeople understand "overnight success" occurs over the course of a lifetime.

Once success is achieved, top salespeople understand success cannot be taken for granted. Efforts sometimes become diffused by thinking success is automatic.

Some become so involved with outside activities they can no longer concentrate on their primary mission. I have known several people who became so deeply involved with outside activities their businesses literally failed.

"I had to run away from home," one successful man told me upon his retirement. "I had become so involved with outside activities, I couldn't escape. I had no choice but to move out of state so I could regain some semblance of organization in my life."

Those of us who enjoy sports are familiar with the

Sports Illustrated curse. When a certain athlete or team is pictured on the front cover, the odds are pretty good the featured athlete or team is headed for a fall.

This happens in business too. Research has shown business performance begins to slide when companies and executives receive public acclaim on magazine covers or are given special awards. Fame often becomes a distraction and results in a lack of focus as they take their eyes off the ball.

In the early 1920s, the Pierce Arrow was the Cadillac (or should I say the Lexus) of the auto industry. In 1921 the president of Pierce Arrow was asked what changes he anticipated making in the 1922 model year, and he said, "None, because we have built a perfect automobile." Chances are you will not see many Pierce Arrows in the parking lot today.

Complacency is an enemy of great salespeople, as is serving on too many boards. Successful people should think long and hard about serving on boards of public companies. Although certainly an honor, directorships have become increasingly time consuming, and the liability associated with such boards has become devastating. More and more directors are being held personally liable for the decisions they make as board members.

While non-profit boards do not present as much liability exposure as for-profit boards, the time commitment can become overwhelming. While it may be a big boost to your self esteem when non-profit organizations ask you to join them because of your awe-inspiring expertise, it's important to remember most non-profit boards are "give and get" boards. They want your involvement because of the money you will *give* and the money you will *get* from others. Sorry to burst your ego bubble. Be very selective when choosing boards on which to serve—one or two in which you have an intense interest. One or two means just that. Then say no.

To Super-Size your sales, write down your goals. Make those goals activity related and not results related. Read them daily. Pursue them with intensity. Stay on course. And don't get discouraged. Success is just around the corner.

NO, NO, NO, NO, NO

How many times do I have to tell you? Absolutely, positively NO!

It should be no surprise every prospective buyer does not buy following every sales presentation. If the sales process were easy, there would be no need for salespeople, only a need for order takers who take the customer's money when a product or service changes hands. This reminds me of how some people in the sales field ply their trade.

I hate to shop, and I avoid it whenever possible. The two exceptions are book stores and hardware stores. I often go into book stores to see what books they have in their special promotion displays and to see if they have one of my books in stock. If I find one of my own books nearly hidden on a bottom shelf with the spine out, I sometimes move it to an eye-level shelf with the cover out so it will sell more quickly. Book store employees must hate people like me because somebody has to put all the books in proper order again.

If I can't find one of my books in stock, I may ask a store employee if they have the book available. When they offer to order it for me, I tell them, "Thank you anyway, but you need not bother. I need a copy right away." Frankly, I'm a pain in the kazootee.

As a hardware store shopper, I'm nearly as troublesome. I love all kinds of new power tools and shop gizmos; however, my shop is already overflowing with neat tools I've never learned how to use. Therefore, the practical side of me usually prevails and I leave the store without buying.

Like many people, I shop occasionally and seldom buy.

When Sylvia insists I accompany her to the mall, I usually find a bench in the mall where I can people watch as she shops. Not long ago, I counted the people who walked by and kept tabs on how many were overweight. I won't give you the percentage, but it was a bunch. And I sometimes count the people who pass by who are not carrying packages. They're shopping, but they're not buying.

If shopping is not a national pastime, it comes close. Packs of high school kids flow by with their friends. Older folks mall-walk to avoid the either too-hot or too-cold weather outside. Often they go into stores to look at merchandise—shopping, but generally not buying.

More people go into the stores merely to peruse the merchandise than actually to buy something.

Why then do so many salespeople think it's a personal insult when prospects do not buy? It's just that salespeople, like most of us, don't like the word "no." High school boys are fearful of the word when they ask a girl for a date;

employees fear the word when they're asking the boss for a raise; I can recall my fear when I asked my wife to marry me, and that was more than 50 years ago. Fear of rejection lingers for a long time.

Successful salespeople understand "no" is not demeaning. It's not shameful or humiliating. The word does not reflect negatively on the salesperson. "No" is a part of life.

"I can't stand the rejection," salespeople often say. "I can't tolerate these…these…these…these…people who come in here and waste my time."

America's most successful salespeople understand every prospect does not buy. This is normal. If every prospect *did* buy, the challenge of the sales profession would be gone. If sales were easy, the profession would attract nearly everyone. And if everybody were in sales, no one would be successful. Easy jobs pay $7.25 an hour. This is not what most people aspire to achieve.

Top salespeople see the value in every contact with every prospect. They see themselves as assistant buyers, representing the interests of the customer. If in fact your product or service best serves the interests of the customer, the odds of a sale increase dramatically.

Nearly every top-ranked salesperson over time has built a tolerance for rejection. In Julie Fenser's book *In the Words of Great Business Leaders*, "Nearly all buyers say 'No' at first. Real salesmen stick until the buyer has used up his last 'No.'"

Sales experts have said a buyer says "no" five times before he or she buys. Obviously it depends upon the product and service being sold, and I've found it's true in my former business when appointing independent agents to represent our company. We were always trying to appoint the very best people we could find. If they were really as good as we thought they were, they didn't need us. They had all the property and casualty insurance markets they needed. On the other hand, if the agent badly needed another market immediately and was anxious to represent us after the first call, we were always suspicious that the agent may not be the quality agent we had thought. After our people had called on one prospective agent over a period of many months, he told us, "I'm getting better service from your company, whom I don't represent, than I receive from the companies I do represent, so I think I'll take you on." A sale often takes time and requires repetition.

Great salespeople are able to see the value in every contact with ever prospect. Even though the prospect doesn't buy today, he or she may buy in the future. I've seen dozens of situations in which a prospect contacts the salesperson, "I talked to you last year, and I've decided I want to do business with you." I've seen many instances in which the sale occurred as much as three to five years after the initial contact.

Patience and a tolerance for rejection will help you *Super-Size Your Sales.*

CUSTOMERS ASK ABOUT PRICE— BUT BUY VALUE

"Okay, okay, okay. You keep talking about this value stuff," a sales person told me not long ago, "but you don't understand. My customers are different. They're interested in only three things—price, price and price."

"We have more competition in this market than anyplace else in the country," another said.

Comments of this type are not uncommon. Most sales people think their situation is different: their customers are different; their markets are different; their competition is different; their economy is different; or something in their sales environment causes prospective customers to focus primarily on price.

"The economy in our town is pretty rough," one salesperson told me. "We have 10% unemployment. People here buy only on the basis of price." (This means only 90% are working).

Whenever a salesperson complains about unemployment in his or her market, I explain that over the past 50 years the normal unemployment rate is about 5%. That is, about 5% of the American people, at any time in recent history, either can't work or won't work; therefore, a 10% unemployment rate is 5% above normal.

Whenever unemployment is an issue, analyze the markets you are serving. As this is being written, one of the largest unemployment categories is teens with an unemployment rate of 26.4%. If you are selling million dollar homes, Mercedes, or other high-end products or services, this is probably not a market you are serving. If most of your clients are college graduates, the unemployment rate is about half the published rate overall.

Don't let the media and the politicians discourage you when unemployment rises or economic problems emerge. Perhaps there are still active markets in the demographic categories you normally serve. To compare your progress, look at only three to five of your best competitors in your industry, and pay attention to your own sales/operations record. In other words, compete with yourself. When things are tough, many of your competitors throw in the towel or sit around chatting with the Maytag repairman "because nobody is buying right now." This opens the door further for salespeople who continue to pursue their sales plan aggressively.

Interestingly, the reasons listed for customers purchasing only on the basis of price are fairly consistent from city to city, from state to state, and even from industry to industry.

Customers Ask About Price—But Buy Value

Yet I've found regardless of the industry, the state, the city, the economy, and the level of competition, certain sales people succeed and prosper while others in those same markets, with the same competition, the same economy, and sometimes even the same prices, struggle and often fail.

The difference is *salespeople who Super-Size their sales add value to the sales transaction.* They sell *value* rather than price.

Most people recognize value in the products or services they buy as consumers. But I've found time and again salespeople who recognize value in the products or services they buy do not recognize value in the products or services they sell.

The reason the importance of value is often overlooked by salespeople is prospective customers often ask about price first, "What will it cost for……..?" It's easy to get the impression price rules.

I pointed out earlier nobody wants to live in the cheapest house, wear the cheapest clothes, eat the cheapest food, or buy anything else that is cheapest. They want quality products and services, and they certainly don't want to be cheated. In fact, people enjoy spending money. Consider the money being spent on pets, such as matching leashes and collars that change with the season, $10,000 diamond studded collars, pictures taken by professional pet photographers, dog resorts, pet therapists, chemotherapy, kidney transplants and MRIs, and special pet clothes and furniture. Your kids and your spouse may be grumpy and disagreeable, but not your pet, and people are willing to pay for that pleasant relationship.

People associate price with quality. A number of studies have shown when prices are increased, people's preference for the product increases. But it's important to remember higher prices also mean higher expectations.

It's essential to remember the issue isn't price but value. The most successful salespeople understand what value really means; they understand how to add value to the products or services they sell; and they understand why consumers mislead by asking about price first.

When we first moved to Florida to escape Ohio's ice and snow, I went to the pharmacy at a drugstore near our home. The pharmacy employees were rude and uncaring. But I thought they may be having a bad day, so I gave them another chance. On my second visit the pharmacy technicians gave me the impression they were graduates of the Barney Frank Charm School, so I decided I wouldn't do business with them again.

I went to the pharmacy of another major drug store chain and said, "It seems to me I'm spending too much for my wife's and my prescriptions," as I handed him a list. "Can you save me any money?"

Why did I mention money? Because I didn't want to explain a competitor was staffed by a kennel of pit bulls.

The pharmacist went to his computer, looked up prices, jotted prices on my list, came back to me and said, "We can't save you any money." With that he turned and walked away. Perhaps he was too busy to sell me on the values his pharmacy could offer, but I doubt that was the case for I was the only customer in the pharmacy at the time. Had he said to me, "Our prices are similar to what you are currently paying, but we offer a number of additional benefits many of our competitors do not have available"—and then name them—very likely I would have done business with this pharmacy.

The reason customers ask about price is they don't know what else to ask—or they don't want to get into the negative experiences they have had with competitors. When

Customers Ask About Price—But Buy Value

customers ask about price, they are really asking, "Where can I get the best value?

In many cases customers ask about price, and dicker over price, because price is the only thing apparent to the untrained eye. Many buyers, at least initially, view most products and services as commodities. That is, they're all the same. In a commodity market, the cheapest price always wins. History tells us no company can make a profit over the long haul by selling commodity products or services. Sooner or later the profit margins will be squeezed so tightly commodity companies can't stay in business. You must prove that your product or service is not a commodity, which means you, the salesperson, must add value.

Someone must explain to buyers why one product better serves the buyers' needs than another—why one service is different and better than that available elsewhere. These values must be explained. The person who does the explaining is the salesperson. Customers are not expected to know the difference between products and services and the values they offer. This is your job.

Here are some of the values a customer looks for:

Why do people move up to bigger, more expensive homes? The most frequent answers fall into the categories of status or prestige, comfort, and convenience to schools and shopping. All these are significant values.

A hotel chain, instead of discounting rooms, came up with a promotion offering a free dinner for every stay. They found perceived value always trumps cheap.

At one time hotels charged $2 a day for each child who slept in the same room. There was also an additional charge for a crib, an extra charge for air conditioning, and an extra charge for a private bath. There was even a coin box on the TV set. Kemmons Wilson, tired of the way travelers were treated, ended these practices. He founded Holiday Inn, named after the Bing Crosby movie, and changed the hotel industry, creating value American consumers soon began to expect.

In tough economic times, will customers revert to cheap instead of value? We'll watch public acceptance of a new low-cost, no frills hotel in London called *easyDorm*. It's a 90 square foot cubicle with a shower, lavatory and floor mattress for $5 a day. You can purchase bedding and toiletries or bring your own. There's an extra charge if you don't do your own cleaning. Frankly, I wouldn't bet on it.

Interestingly, today the airlines are doing what the hotel industry used to do. They're making an extra charge to check a bag, for a blanket or pillow, for an aisle or exit seat, Internet service, and priority boarding, while the airlines watch their customer approval ratings plummet.

Elegant restaurants create value with ambiance and good service. Good food doesn't even make the top of the list. People see candlelight, soft music, pleasant surroundings, and elegant service as value they're willing to pay for.

Nearly any new car represents value to the buyer. Status, prestige and comfort generally represent even greater value. That's why dealers sell more expensive cars than inexpensive ones.

Why are most cars sold on Friday nights, Saturdays and Sundays? Convenience. More people have time available over the weekend to shop for a major purchase. There's a lot going on in the American economy after normal working hours, and it's up to those of us in the sales business to be available when America wants to do business, not when *we* want to do business. Convenience translates to value.

Convenience is a factor in nearly every purchase. More

Customers Ask About Price—But Buy Value

than half of the gross receipts of fast food restaurants are taken in through the drive-through window. It's more convenient. And the trend started largely because of child seats. When you get a kid in a car seat, you don't get him out easily.

Convenience is also a reason fast-food restaurants are accepting credit cards. It's more convenient for the restaurant too. It speeds up the payment process to about five seconds. Cash requires eight to ten seconds.

I entered the property and casualty insurance business in 1958 in the small town of Fort Scott, Kansas. The company, by far the largest employer in town, was located in the center of downtown. You could walk a couple of blocks to either end of Main Street where most of the merchants were located. The core hours of my employer ended at 5 p.m, the same time downtown stores closed.

Occasionally, however, one of the insurance company employees would leave the company and enter one of the stores before the merchant had an opportunity to lock the doors. And you can't believe the despicable behavior these folks displayed; they tried to buy something!

Obviously, this form of unacceptable conduct could not continue, so the merchants started locking the doors at ten minutes before five so the insurance people wouldn't come in and try to buy something at closing time. "You can come back when it's convenient for me to sell you something, not necessarily when it's convenient for you to buy," the merchants seemed to suggest.

This worked out well for several years, until Walmart built a store at the edge of town and remained open until 11 o'clock at night, including Saturdays, Sundays and holidays.

Today most of the merchants in that small town are out of business, and the remaining merchants are struggling at best and cussing Sam Walton. And I maintain Sam Walton didn't cause their downfall. They did it to themselves by failing to provide a valued customer service, remaining open when it was convenient for the customer, not necessarily convenient for the seller.

In those early days Walmart did not have a price advantage. They did not build a store near a K-Mart because Sam Walton believed he could not compete with K-Mart prices, so he offered convenient hours and friendly service. A greeter smiled and spoke to customers and directed them to the proper aisle for the item they were looking for. And associates were asked to smile and speak to customers if within ten feet, the Walton Ten-Foot Rule, ignored for the most part today. Sam would not be happy.

Instant service is a value American consumers insist upon. Consumers don't like to wait. A friend told me he had gone to the supermarket to do his grocery shopping. Only one checkout station was open, with a line of 14 people, most with large baskets of groceries. Several customers left their filled baskets sitting in the store rather than to wait in line. The store had failed to fill a critical customer need.

I nearly always pull for the underdog. When K-Mart first took bankruptcy, I made a special effort to shop there whenever I thought they might have what I needed. One day I found the item I wanted, proceeded to the checkout counter and found not a single checkout was open. I asked a young lady working near the front of the store, "How do you buy something here?" and she told me I should go to the customer service counter. There I found one clerk who was waiting on a customer trying to return something without a receipt.

I stuck it out. But soon there was one, two and finally

Customers Ask About Price—But Buy Value

a five-person line behind me; these customers pushed their baskets aside and left the store. The American people want instant service and will go elsewhere if necessary to get it.

Everybody hates lines. One survey shows long checkout lines cost more business sales every day than any other single factor. Customer satisfaction takes a nose-dive the longer people have to wait.

Most people are not well acquainted with the insurance business and, therefore, prefer to work with an agent. They want a professional who understands the business to help them make decisions on what insurance coverages are needed and to help them get the best value. They want to do business with people in whom they have trust and confidence. They get comfort in dealing with a professional on whom they feel they can depend. And there's even greater comfort when there's a claim and the local professional is there to help. American people choose a doctor or lawyer for the same reason—they want pros who know the business and who inspire the values of trust and confidence.

Not long ago I fired my personal physician who was routinely rude, uncaring and arrogant. He may have been the best doctor in the world, but I prefer a doctor who makes the call as pleasant as possible.

The reasons people buy higher priced coffee parallels the reasons they buy most other products. The most frequent answers are: convenience, service, flavor (even though everyone starts with the same coffee bean), relationships (customers like the personnel in certain restaurants), and prestige. All these are values American consumers expect.

Starbucks Chairman Howard Schultz attributes Starbucks success to "quality of coffee, soft seating, design, music and social atmosphere," creating an "experience," a "third place" outside home and work. He says the "social atmosphere, the romance, all of these things are as relevant in Singapore and China as they are in Zurich or Seattle."

My point should be obvious. Buyers consistently choose value over price. People choose to buy products or services based primarily on prestige, comfort, convenience, ambiance, service, confidence, trust, and relationships, regardless of the product or service being purchased.

Review your own purchasing decisions over the past 30 days or so and see how these factors affected your purchases. In how many cases did you buy the cheapest product or service available? We've done this in the Bailey family many times, and we find quality and service nearly always trump low cost.

Studies show that in most cases sale prices do not increase sales over the longer pull. A sale simply pulls sales from future periods. They buy now rather than next month. That's why super-successful salespeople concentrate on value rather than price.

In my former business, property and casualty insurance, some 300 to 500 insurance companies are competing for any one line of insurance in most states. What are the odds any one company is going to have the lowest price over the long pull? Insurance rates are a leapfrog situation. The company having the lowest price today is almost certain to lose that position tomorrow. On any given day it is likely several competitors are changing rate levels. Therefore, over a period of years, price generally becomes relatively insignificant. Value, however, does not become insignificant.

Sales people who sell on price will often lose the customer for the same reason. Sell on price, lose on price.

Customers Ask About Price—But Buy Value

The unsuccessful sales person doesn't understand how to create value and tries to sell price. The successful sales person, on the other hand, does not sell price but sells value.

When a customer asks, "What's this going to cost?" he or she means, "Am I getting good value for my money?" You can bet they'll ask about price. But they'll buy value—almost always. And top salespeople who Super-Size their sales can explain those values convincingly.

TELL TWO PEOPLE

Earlier in this book I told you every customer can be worth multi-millions of dollars to you. It's an undisputed fact and the most powerful principle in the sales field, yet too few recognize it.

Let's say your next customer is totally pleased with you as a salesperson and with the product and service you have provided. As a result, tomorrow he or she tells two people about you. The next day each of those two people tells two people; and the next day each of those two people tells two people; etc. How many people will you reach in 30 days?

The answer is 536,870,912 people.

There are about 300 million people in the United State. That means *nearly every man, woman and child in the United States will receive your message twice over the next 30 days*. It's an astonishing number. If you are mathematically inclined, you may wish to check my math.

Tell Two People

Of course, it can be argued not everyone will tell two people. Some will undoubtedly break the chain. But giving overwhelming service and building a great relationship with a customer is not a one-time event. By giving truly outstanding service to every single customer—and practicing the principles we have discussed in this book for every single customer—the "tell two people" principle is initiated many times over the course of a day. The number of people who hear about you is even more dramatic.

The primary reason companies are overwhelmingly successful is that customers tell others. And likewise this is the primary reason companies fail. As a matter of fact, negative experiences are passed on more readily than positive experiences, especially in this email world where it's easy to pass along horrible experiences to an entire address book. Few companies that treat customers poorly can survive very long. And companies that *always* treat customers well are nearly universally successful.

The most successful insurance agents tell me their primary marketing technique is "word of mouth." Simply put, happy customers tell others about their favorable experience.

Word-of-mouth campaigns, sometimes called buzz marketing, are not just for small mom and pop businesses. They work for big businesses too. Some large organizations have formally organized such campaigns to get through the clutter of about 250 television channels and to reach a generation obsessed with video games and surfing the Internet. Also, these campaigns are cheaper than paid advertising.

Jaguar has provided cars free of charge to a number of people who are seen in the right restaurants and night spots in major cities with the hope others will want to emulate that lifestyle. Procter and Gamble has recruited some

600,000 mothers to pass out coupons and talk-up new products. They select moms who speak to 25 to 30 other women during the day, while the average mom talks to five. Kellogg and Chrysler likewise have formalized programs of asking loyal customers to tell others about their products.

Companies pay kids to wear their clothes, drink their beverages, eat their food, ride their scooters, play their games, read their books, and smoke their cigarettes, in the hope other kids will want to be like them. They aren't supposed to tell anybody they're getting paid, although the newly formed Word of Mouth Marketing Association—WOMMA—requires full disclosure.

A NASA engineer and some buddies as a lark formed a Web site called usbeerdrinkingteam.com, and it has generated hundreds of thousands of members. They hope to register a significant number of the 90 million beer drinkers in the U. S.

People have incredible influence on others. Psychologists tell us some 90% of us follow the crowd.

No form of advertising or marketing is more genuine or believable than a recommendation from a satisfied customer or someone who personally knows the salesperson. Customers become evangelists for the outstanding product or the overwhelming service they received.

Research has shown the sales closing ratio drops significantly when the customer was not referred by a satisfied customer. It increases to about 60% when a friend or satisfied customer refers the prospect to the salesperson.

How you treat your next customer—and every customer—over time creates a recognized brand name that can rank well with the outstanding brand names in America. *You* become a respected and well-known brand name.

Coca-Cola is perhaps the most recognized brand name in the nation, maybe the world. Coca-Cola is sold in more than 200 countries. About nine million stores sell some 1.2 billion Cokes a day.

Other famous brands include Microsoft, IBM, GE, Disney, McDonald's, Mercedes, KFC, Pizza Hut, Kodak, and Taco Bell. In China the most recognized brand is KFC, ahead of Coke and McDonald's.

Harley-Davidson is a global brand. And who doesn't yearn for a Porsche? What a brand name!

BMW and Mercedes have built brand names on the smallest of details—the pitch of the engine, the sound of warning buzzers, the glove box lid, wiper motors and turn signals. Your brand name is built on small details too.

Once a positive brand has been established, it has tremendous value and staying power. Indian Motorcycles stopped production in 1953. A number of attempts have been made to resurrect the Indian. In 1999 the trademark, just the name, sold for $22 million.

When business people buy a franchise, they buy a brand name that provides instant name recognition. A business reputation is associated with that name, good or bad.

Several years ago insurance agency franchising came into vogue. A very successful insurance agent who represented my former company called and asked for my advice on buying a franchise. "Who is better known and has the most favorable reputation in your city," I asked, "you or XYZ Insurance, the franchiser?"

"I am," he responded without hesitation.

"I agree," I answered, "so maybe they should pay you a fee for your reputation rather than your paying them." Not every franchise provides for the franchisee the desired name recognition and a favorable business reputation. Just one poor franchisee, or even one instance of poor service, can taint a brand name forever. Greg Stielstra, in his book *PyroMarketing*, says 96% of buyers will switch from their favorite brand if they receive greater value at the same price elsewhere.

About 35 years ago our family stayed at a well-known hotel in Atlanta while returning from a Florida vacation. That night was one of our most horrible experiences. We have never stayed in a hotel in this chain since, although there are probably many good ones. I'm certain we have driven many unnecessary miles and maybe spent more money than necessary simply to avoid this particular brand. A tarnished brand name has negative value. And just one unfavorable customer experience can have a harmful effect for a lifetime.

A scandal can destroy a brand within days. Perrier lost some 60% of its market several years ago when traces of benzene were found in its bottled water.

Because of an accounting scandal, Anderson Consulting felt the need to change its name to Accenture. CBS, which once "owned" a third of the television market, has lost much of its viewing audience as some 200 to 250 channels diluted the market and as its reputation became damaged by high profile news bias. The public is not very forgiving.

Well-known brands are no guarantee of success. Philip Morris changed its name to Altria. Electrolux is now Aerus. Polaroid, once a solid brand, became a victim of technology and filed for bankruptcy. International Harvester is now Novartis; and ValueJet became AirTran. The Firestone brand was tarnished when tires on Ford cars had to be recalled. By failing to take voluntary action quickly to correct known problems with certain tire models, Firestone paid a high price, and the company was purchased by Bridgestone in 1988.

Even the state of North Dakota, in effect a well-known brand, once considered dropping the word "North" from its name, becoming just plain Dakota. Why change? Because the brand was synonymous with cold weather, making it less appealing to tourists and businesses.

Brands have value when customers know what to expect. The brand represents quality, cleanliness, and consistency in every phase of business operations. If there's not consistency from location to location and from customer to customer, the brand name may have negative value. A few bad apples can ruin the entire barrel.

The real brand value depends primarily on *you* and your actions. Advertising is not the common denominator of creating an effective brand. Despite multi-million dollar advertising programs, can you name the current advertising slogans of Coke? (No, it's not "It's the Real Thing" - 1969 or "I'd Like to Teach the World to Sing" – 1971). McDonald's? Wendy's? Miller Lite? I can't, and I've asked several others as this is being written, and they can't either.

During the Super Bowl, there is nearly as much hype about the commercials as there is about the game. Yet many viewers can remember the commercial but cannot remember the name of the advertiser. This is not a terrific business investment, especially when a 30 second commercial costs millions of dollars. None of us can rely on advertising to create the brand image to which we aspire.

Even great brands sometimes lose value when competitors follow with similar products. Sanka produced the first decaf coffee. When people wanted decaf, they asked for Sanka. Today every coffee company makes decaf, and most restaurants still use the bright orange Sanka color on the decaf coffee carafes. Unfortunately for Sanka, they receive no value from its well-established brand. At one time all refrigerators were Frigidaires. (Would you get the milk out of the Frigidaire?) Today all tissues are Kleenex; all mending tape is Scotch; all Q-Tips are, well, Q-Tips;

all crawler tractors are Caterpillar; and all copy machines are Xerox. (Just a minute while I Xerox this page on my HP copier).

There are living brands as well. Oprah. Martha. You know the last names without my using them.

When something happens to cause the public to dislike the living brand, they turn away from the product or service as well. For instance, O. J. Simpson and Hertz. Dell Computer dumped its TV spokesman, "Steven," after he was arrested for possession of marijuana. Tiger has lost several sponsors.

And sometimes the public doesn't connect the ad or spokesperson with the product or service. The sponsor of the Energizer Bunny is often confused, and credit was often given to Burger King instead of Wendy's for Clara Peller's "Where's the Beef" commercial.

To build an effective brand, some argue, there must be some mystique surrounding the name, like Starbucks, which has become not just a brand but a lifestyle, complete with comfortable seating and light jazz.

But America's most successful salespeople know their actions, their relationship with the next customer and every customer, create respected brands that work for them 24/7. They know their brands, their reputations and their names, are fragile and one slip-up can wreck a lifetime of work. It's easy to list the names of politicians whose careers have ended because of personal transgressions. It seems they never learn.

Your name is an implicit promise of quality. "John Jones always provides high-quality products and service to his customers."

Your name exudes a feeling of trust, comfort, security, convenience and service. "Judy Smith takes care of her customers. I know I can depend on her."

Your name narrows down the field, making the buying decision easier. "The ads and the Internet sites are confusing. I think I'll stick with Jill Brown. I know I can't go wrong with her."

Your name has the power to command a premium price. "Bill Cooper may charge a little more, but I know I always get more value from him."

Movie stars say, "Give me press. I don't care if it's good press or bad press. Just give me press." This may work for movie stars, but only positive name recognition and an unblemished reputation works for great salespeople.

Your personal brand is worth multi-millions of dollars. It starts with your next customer and is passed on to some 536,870,912 people, the real key to Super-Sizing your sales.

LISTEN

Several times during my career I've had interviews with prospective employers who seemed to have the roles reversed. They talked so much about themselves and their companies they had little opportunity to learn about me, the potential new employee. It was as if I were interviewing them.

Amateur salespeople tend to do the same. They think their job entails talking, so they talk. And they talk. They sound like a new car pitchman on TV, screaming about the good deals they are offering. They repeat every canned sales blurb they've ever read about, thinking the next statement will seal the deal. Talking too much leaves the potential buyer turned off, frustrated and anxious to end the discussion so he or she can buy elsewhere. Sometimes they keep selling after the sale is made until they un-sell the sale.

LISTEN

As we discussed earlier, America's most successful salespeople are problem solvers. And if problems are to be solved, the salespeople must understand what the problems are. Understanding customer needs comes from listening during a "sales conversation," which is different from a social conversation. Listen—learn the needs of the prospect. Don't interrupt. Ask questions to learn what you can do to serve the client. When the customer's needs are fully understood, then and only then, explain how you can meet those needs.

Great salespeople listen at least 80% of the time. They ask questions the other 20%. They are themselves. They sell from the heart, not with their vocal chords.

Research has shown when the product or service is matched more precisely to the individual needs of the buyer, customers will spend 5% to 10% more than they would spend otherwise. Those needs are determined by listening.

Through listening, the salesperson may determine the needs of the prospect cannot be best met with his or her products or services. Great salespeople say, "I'm sorry, but other companies can better meet your needs," and then they make a recommendation.

Although the public probably sees all property and casualty insurance companies in the same light, they're all different. There are companies that specialize in auto or home; others specialize in workers' compensation, boats, aircraft, etc. Run of the mill agents, in the interest of receiving a commission, may try to force a certain type of policy into a company that doesn't have the appetite or experience to handle it properly. Great agents, on the other hand, will refer the account to an insurer that can best serve the policyholder.

The same is true in other industries. Companies specialize in different products, services, or demographic categories.

Some companies have spent big bucks to employ "empathy consultants" to help salespeople learn how to identify with customers' feelings and needs and to develop favorable relationships with customers.

The listening approach should also be used to handle irate customers. Ask a question, and another question. I've done this hundreds of times through the years, and I can say it works without exception. When irate customers come to you, they have already decided beforehand you are going to be unfair. When you ask questions without being judgmental, they soon change their opinion and begin to decide, "Maybe this guy (or gal) is going to be fair with me after all."

Once they describe the situation that has upset them, ask, "When did this occur?" The next question might be, "Was anyone with you at the time?" Continue the questioning technique, without sharing your own opinion, until all possible facts have been expressed. Then you can say, "Here's how we normally handle situations like this." Or if further investigations are necessary, say, "I'll have one of our people check into this and we'll get back to you tomorrow morning." Then make sure someone in fact follows through.

Listening helps you put yourself in the clients' shoes.

Listening helps you build relationships and trust. Customers won't buy from you if they don't trust you.

Listening helps you build rapport with the customer.

Listening helps you align yourself with the interests of the customer.

Listening is another critical building block to help you *Super-Size Your Sales*.

WHY SHOULD I BUY FROM YOU?

When speaking to sales groups throughout the country, I often ask, "Why should I buy from you? And don't use the word 'service' in your answer."

It's surprising how salespeople struggle for an answer, even salespeople who have been in the business for years. Many simply haven't given much thought to the question.

The reason I ask the word "service" not be used in the answer is most salespeople answer by saying, "I give good customer service." As a matter of fact, I have never talked to a salesperson who *said* he or she did not give good customer service, even though I know many do not. I know from personal experience and from talking with thousands of buyers throughout the country, customers generally express disappointment with the service they receive from many firms, possibly *most* firms.

America's most successful salespeople are able to reel off dozens of valid reasons customers should buy from them. They don't necessarily share all the reasons with every customer. They may use only one or two, just the reasons that apply specifically to the problem or problems of that particular client. Or they may not use any at all. As great salespeople gain experience, they exude so much confidence that customers sense the values they are gaining from doing business with the top pros. And in many cases the reputations of great salespeople have already established those values in the minds of many, if not most, prospective buyers.

Still, all salespeople should develop lists of reasons customers should buy from them. Keep the items short, simple, specific, and easy to understand. Not only will these reasons be helpful for the customer, but they also build confidence in the minds of the salespeople themselves. If salespeople have no confidence in themselves, certainly buyers cannot have confidence in them. The salesperson who says, "I can't sell because my price is too high" has no confidence in the other values he or she can add to the transaction.

Without knowing your business and without knowing more about you specifically, I can't build your list of reasons buyers should buy from you. But here are examples of values added by top-tier salespeople.

Travel agents have been hurt financially as airlines continue to cut commissions and as more people buy airline tickets online. Yet some agents are prospering by specializing and by providing overwhelming service and knowledge of some segment of the travel experience.

One travel counselor says, "We've been marketing ourselves as 'we're free' when we should have been promoting the special values we add to the travel experience". Some agencies are specializing in particular destinations: Australia, Switzerland, Hawaii, and other points around the world. One handles only professional tennis players and charges $300 per hour for its services. Another specializes in chartering private jets. One specializes in renting castles. Still another specializes in adventure travel, such as running with the bulls in Pamplona, scouting Incan ruins in Peru or trekking in Tibet.

These specialty firms can tell you which picturesque villages to visit, which restaurants to seek out, and which cathedrals are worthy of a visit. And they're charging for it—from $250 to $500 per person per trip.

Of the approximately 250,000 travel agents selling travel in about 32,000 retail agency locations, some 10,000 have become travel counselors. Like salespeople in so many industries, about 4% are prospering as top-tier producers.

As a frequent traveler for both business and personal purposes, I can tell you with certainty the services my travel agency provides are well worth the modest fee it charges. They find better deals than I can find on my own. And when problems emerge, which is not uncommon in travel, they can work them out far better than I can. I have to admit in most cases I arrange my own air travel on the Internet. But in far too many cases I wish I had not when, for instance, there is a last minute schedule change I have trouble unraveling. The involvement of a pro would have been worth the small fee involved.

Why should you buy from me? Because we are experts in a specific travel experience. We know the best restaurants, the best condos, the site-seeing experiences you shouldn't miss. Our people have been there. They know the location first hand.

If you're in the entertainment business in Orlando, you're going to have competition—tough competition—from Disney World, Universal Studios and Sea World. How can you compete? Avoid the thing people dislike most about Disney and some of the other vacation destinations—long lines.

The answer is Discovery Cove, a 30 acre park where visitors have unlimited access to hundreds of species of exotic birds, can snorkel alongside graceful rays and hundreds of tropical fish, can enjoy long stretches of white sand beaches, and can swim with the amazing bottlenose dolphin. This is an unforgettable place because it has lots of personal space and no long lines. Only 1,000 people are admitted each day. The admission price includes snacks and beverages throughout the day.

Why should you buy from us? Because you'll have the time of your life, and there are no lines and no crowds.

Disney has tackled the long-line problem with its Fastpass program. And they've eliminated other problems that can ruin a vacation. Every year some 20,000 people lose their cars in the Disney World parking lots; about 5,000 people a year lock their keys in their cars.

Disney employees in golf carts help people find their cars. They ask about make, model and license number, but some people don't know because they're rental cars. Then they ask about the approximate arrival time at the park. They check their computer and find at that particular hour they were parking in a certain row in a certain lot. The guest gets in the golf cart with the Disney employee and together they find the car.

For lock-in situations, Disney personnel get the VIN number of the car and have arrangements with manufacturers to have keys made on the spot.

Why should you buy from us? You'll have a wonderful

time at Disney World—and we do everything possible to make the Disney visit a pleasant one.

Some of the customers of a suburban New York men's clothing store call it "the world's most expensive cup of coffee." Yes, prices are high, but customers keep coming back.

Why? Sales people are allowed considerable leeway to go the extra mile for a customer. There are emergency fittings—at home or at the office. One customer was in Japan and unexpectedly had to attend a funeral, but he didn't have a suit. The store called around to find a corporate jet that might be flying to Japan. A suit arrived in time for the funeral.

When a customer shows up at the store, suits, ties and accessories are already laid out for inspection. There are bagels, coffee, friendly chitchat and camaraderie. There are toys for the kids to play with.

They have computer profiles of all 40,000 customers, a list of everything each customer has purchased, nicknames, hobbies, and whatever else is necessary to keep the focus on the customer.

Their only marketing program occurs twice a year at 5:30 a.m. when the owners hang out at local train stations and hand out free coffee, brochures and copies of the *New York Times*.

Why should you buy from us? Because we do whatever it takes to make sure you get top-notch products and overwhelming service.

Several weeks ago Sylvia and I were attending a party when a local optometrist approached and said he had heard me speak about customer service at an event more than a year earlier. "After hearing you speak," he said, "I decided I wasn't giving very good customer service. I had been closing my office at 4:30 p.m., and this irritated many of my patients because they work during the day. So I decided to remain open until 8:00 p.m. on Wednesdays.

"As a result of this one change, my revenues increased about 20%, and my calendar for Wednesday evening appointments is full for more than three months. Now I'm adding the second evening schedule, and I anticipate another 20% revenue increase."

Why should you buy from me? Because I'm a competent optometrist who offers convenient evening hours.

What about you? Develop your own list. Start each benefit with "you," the customer, and list the specific benefits you offer, without using the overworked term "service." Here are a few ideas to help you get started.

You are provided with products of outstanding quality.

You receive the benefit of our expertise at no additional charge. We are experts and know this business thoroughly.

You receive two hour service or even "instant" service.

You can be assured we always do what we say we're going to do when we say we're going to do it.

You can reach me when you need me 24/7. You have my home phone and cell phone numbers.

You don't get a runaround with phone mail. You talk to real human beings.

Start developing your list of reasons why I should buy from you—and don't use the word "service" in your answers. Get ready to *Super-Size Your Sales*.

PERFECT EQUALITY

The last time I checked, there were 24 hours in a day and seven days in a week. Everybody has exactly the same amount of time available. There is no discrimination. You as a salesperson have as much time available as any other salesperson in the world.

Strangely, some people can accomplish 10 times, 20 times, 50 times more than others within the same amount of time. With salespeople, the range of disparity is especially wide because salespeople often control their own schedules to a greater degree than people in other fields. Nobody is looking over the salesperson's shoulder every few minutes insisting certain things be done.

"Time is the only commodity we deal with which cannot be counterfeited, stolen or placed in inventory," says

Zig Ziglar, the popular public speaker. "Remember, time is irreplaceable." Overwhelmingly successful salespeople have learned how to utilize this irreplaceable asset and get more done in the time available.

Here is a story of Bob who makes his living as a salesman—just a living, not a life of luxury. Bob, like so many of us, lacks personal discipline. Here's a typical day in Bob's life:

I think I'll catch a little of the 11 o'clock news to see if anything interesting is going on in the world. After all, as a salesperson, I need to be on top of all the latest developments.

Maybe I'll watch the Tonight Show monolog, just for a couple of minutes. I can't stay up too late because I've got a big day planned tomorrow. Wow! The monolog is especially funny tonight. And the first guest is one of my favorites. Maybe I'll watch a little bit of that segment.

Well, midnight is not really late. I'm young and vigorous and don't need eight hours sleep. I'll get up early tomorrow morning and hit the ground running!

Gee, I can't believe the alarm is going off so early. I think I'll shut it off and stay in bed for just a few more minutes. Besides, it's dark outside. There won't be anybody up and around to sell this time of day anyway.

How could I have gone back to sleep? I'll just skip breakfast and get started on my work day. I've got a lot to do today.

This car is a thousand miles overdue for an oil change. I'll drop it off at the service station on the way to work. I'll still make it to the office by 10. I'll pick up the morning paper at the service station. After all, my clients expect me to stay abreast of what's going on in the world.

What's this? I can't believe my alma mater made the NCAA final four! They started the season with three straight losses. This is fantastic! I think I'll call Larry and badger him a bit. His college is a bitter rival of my college.

I wish I hadn't skipped breakfast this morning. I'm beginning to feel hungry. I think I'll go down to the break room and pick up a donut and cup of coffee.

There are a couple of calls to return, including calls to Art, Bill and Fred to set up a tee time for Saturday morning.

It's almost lunchtime already. It's too near lunch to make a sales call, so maybe I'll have lunch a little early and get moving with a heavy schedule right after lunch.

Would you believe it? I went into this restaurant and ran into Ray and Mel, two old friends I hadn't seen for years. And these guys are as excited about the NCAA tournament as I am. So maybe lunch hour was a little longer than I had planned, but the day is still young. I'll just work later this evening.

Back to the office at 2:00. There were a couple of calls to return. The tee time is set for 7:30 a.m. Saturday. My eye appointment is at 10:00 a.m. Wednesday.

Judy, one of our office associates, is leaving today for maternity leave. There was a baby shower at lunchtime. Maybe I'd better go by her desk and give her my regards.

A stack of mail had accumulated, so I'll just plow through it. About 90% is junk that promptly hits the round file. Action is required on a half dozen items. I'll just route these to the proper people in the office for follow through.

Gosh, it's 4 p.m. And I haven't even checked my e-mail. And what a mess—69 new messages. Fortunately, 52 of them are junk which I can delete immediately.

I thought I'd work late today, but I'm tired. I'll put in an especially long day tomorrow.

I arrive home at 5:30 p.m. My wife asks, "Honey, how did your day go?"

"Am I tired! I was really busy today. This sales business is tough. The economy is horrible."

Far fetched? Maybe a little, but not that much. Salespeople who are not successful (and most other unsuccessful people as well) let time control them rather than their controlling time.

Bob is the type of guy who says he gives 100% to his job—12% on Monday, 23% on Tuesday......

Someone once referred to this phenomenon as the "carnivorous desk." I can't remember the source of the term, but it's a good illustration of what happens to many salespeople. Carnivorous plants attract insects with sweet-smelling nectars and bright colors. They trap the animal life with a sticky substance on the leaves of the plant. Then an enzyme breaks down the body of the insect so the plant can digest it. The carnivorous desk traps and eats its prey in the same manner, tempting the sales person with coffee, friendly conversation, and pleasant surroundings; holds its prey with unnecessary correspondence, e-mail, and non-productive routine activities; and then consumes its prey with failure as a sales person.

Let's replay the day for Jim, a highly effective salesperson.

Jim had dinner with his family—together, sitting down at one time, with the TV set off. He spent some time with the kids, talking about school and helping them with a few homework questions. The kids were in bed by 8:30. Jim and his wife had an hour to talk without interruption about their day.

To bed by 9:30 p.m. If there was a special TV program in which they were especially interested, they taped it for viewing early the next evening or over the weekend.

There was no 11 o'clock news on TV. They'll get their

news from tomorrow morning's newspaper.

The alarm was set for 5:30 a.m.—a solid eight hours sleep. He reminds himself often optimists get up early; pessimists get up late.

Jim and his wife had breakfast together. Jim scanned the morning paper for noteworthy news. He was off to the office by 7. He was at his desk by 7:30.

He completed the paperwork that had accumulated on his desk since yesterday morning.

Judy, his administrative assistant, arrived at 8. She sorted out the junk mail and the routine transactions to be handled by others. Only a half dozen transactions needed Jim's attention. Jim gave instructions to Judy on these items.

By 8:30 Judy had started to sift through Jim's e-mails, zapping the junk. Judy handled those she could and forwarded a few e-mails to Jim for his attention. Jim handled these by 9.

Then Jim worked on sales calls from 9:00 to noon, in a 1-2-3 priority order There was a business lunch at 12 Judy had set up for him. (It was a business lunch—Jim had learned early in his career lunch meetings had to have a legitimate business purpose. Lunch with co-workers or friends seldom can be justified as having a legitimate business purpose).

There were sales appointments from 1:30 to 4:30 that Judy had arranged, again following the priority order he had established before he left work yesterday.

Then back to the office by 5 to see if there was anything requiring his attention before heading home. And he wrote down his sales objectives for tomorrow—numbering them 1-2-3, etc. The highest priority items had the highest payback potential.

He arrived home at about six for dinner with his family.

"How was your day today, dear?"

"I had a great day! Sold three new accounts. What happened in your life today?"

Jim has personal discipline, as is the case for other very successful people. He has clear goals and a burning intensity to achieve those goals. He recognizes the difference between busyness and business. He makes sure six to seven hours of the work day are committed to high-priority sales activities—*real* sales activities, not to paperwork and activities not having payback potential.

Jim is focused on sales, and he uses his time wisely on activities that produce sales. Jim makes an excellent living and is an exceptional provider for his family.

Jim is successful because he makes good use of the 24 hours a day he has available. His personal discipline has enabled him to Super-Size his sales.

Although Bob and Jim are fictional characters, both represent characteristics we find in abundance within the American business world. And that's especially the case within the sales world where salespeople tend to have great discretion in the use of their time.

How about you? Are you a Bob or a Jim?

And what about your customer? Does your customer respect you as a well-organized professional, one who utilizes personal time efficiently and likewise respects the customer's time? I often run into salespeople whom I like personally and who are pleasant people to be around, but they require two hours to perform a 15 minute job. I generally try to avoid people who waste my time.

What about you? Does time control you? Or do you control your time?

PACKAGING

Millions of dollars are spent on designing a package for a new product. Sales executives know if the package isn't attractive and appropriate, the product won't sell, no matter how good it is.

Very successful salespeople know the importance of packaging too. The salesperson is the product. And his or her dress is the package.

This is an often overlooked factor in this casual dress world—a world in which business attire transitioned to casual Fridays, which gradually shifted to casual everyday, which over time became sloppy every day.

According to a *Sales and Marketing Management Magazine* survey, 94% of executives said a sloppily dressed sales rep had a tougher time making a sale, and 80% said they would avoid hiring a sales rep who did not dress appropriately. My own business experience confirms it—people who do not dress well do not perform well. An unpopular position? I know, but it's true nevertheless.

Chances are you wouldn't stop at a restaurant with dirty windows or trash in the parking lot. Theoretically this has nothing to do with the quality of food, but in reality we know there's a relationship. The appearance of the restaurant is a symbol of how management views all dimensions of operations. If the restaurant management doesn't care about trash in the parking lot, which customers *can* see, how are they going to view filth in the kitchen, which customers *can't* see? It's not likely attention will be given to good food and good service without giving attention to cleanliness and general appearance throughout.

Similarly, a salesperson who does not give attention to appearance will not be perceived as an individual who knows the business well and one who is able to give professional service. Most buyers believe casual dress is a symbol of a casual attitude. On the other hand, looking good means good.

This is not to say every successful salesperson must wear a dark suit and tie. Obviously it depends on the product and service being sold, but a good rule of thumb is to dress as your client *expects* you to dress. Emulate the look of your client, and upgrade that look just a bit. It's better to be overdressed than underdressed.

Salespeople in a large Texas insurance agency specialize by industry. Each salesperson is assigned to two specific industries. They dress like the pros in their specific industries. Those who call on executives of major corporations, lawyers, doctors and the like wear suits and ties. Those who call on contractors wear Dockers and a neat collared shirt with no tie.

Tattoos, piercings and hairstyles are a part of the package. Some argue they have this right of individual expression, so they have 25 pounds of hardware hanging from their ears and eyebrows and have so many holes in their body they whistle when they walk (if they ever walk very fast—which isn't likely). Their shoulder-length hair would be a challenge to comb with a garden rake. Perhaps it is a right, but it's not a right for people who intend to be truly successful. Buyers simply won't buy from people who look like this (unless they're buying tattoos and piercings).

Employee discrimination suits are being brought against employers because of guidelines on personal appearance, tattoos, piercings, and hairstyles; therefore, an employer must be cautious about the nature of personal appearance guidelines established for employees. But for the very successful salesperson, and the person who aspires to be one, guidelines do not matter. They know they will simply not be successful unless they present a professional appearance.

Less than professional dress adversely affects performance in many ways. Some believe casual dress has had the effect of reducing the normal workweek by 20%. One firm strenuously argues business improved 30% to 40% by eliminating casual Fridays. There is some evidence casually dressed workers are more error prone. One firm found casual dress increased tardiness, absenteeism and flirtatious behavior. Teachers found that student behavior deteriorated on dress-down Fridays.

A popular morning radio talk show host, now retired, once broadcast from his apartment high above the City of Columbus, Ohio. He was in his own apartment—nobody was around—so he felt it didn't matter how he dressed. He often sat down behind the mike in his pajamas.

But he could feel something was wrong. He felt his delivery didn't have the enthusiasm, the excitement, the zest for which he was noted. He asked the radio production people if they had detected a difference. They had. And some listeners had already expressed the same concern.

He started to wear a collared dress shirt with tie and no jacket—the way he had dressed when he broadcast from the radio studio. The vibrant, energetic personality was back. He could feel the difference—and his listeners felt it too.

Many argue professional business dress is old fashioned. Nevertheless, the nation's most successful salespeople know professional dress inspires confidence, both in the buyer and the salesperson, and establishes buyer trust—a huge sales advantage. Keeping trim and fit is also a part of the package.

Salespeople who reach the top always look the part. They know the package is as important as the product.

How does your customer view your package? If you are to *Super-Size Your Sales*, the customer should be inspired by your attire and have confidence in you because of your professional dress. Your attire will give you greater confidence too.

DOES ANYBODY CARE?

A few years ago Sylvia and I were searching for a new home. We worked with a very capable realtor. She appeared to know her business and was very professional in every regard—except one. When lunch time rolled around, she pulled into a restaurant parking lot, parked in a slot reserved for the handicapped, took a handicapped tag from her glove compartment, and placed it on the rear view mirror. She appeared to be trying to provide extraordinary customer service for us. We had to take only a few steps to the front door of the restaurant with little exposure to the weather.

When we arrived at our hotel room that evening, almost immediately Sylvia and I asked each other the same question: "Should we be dealing with this realtor? If she'll cheat by using a handicapped tag, can we trust her with other matters?"

How important is ethics in sales when widespread ethics abuses are all around us? We tend to rationalize our conduct by saying, "Everybody does it." Certainly ethics violations are widespread.

Employees nearly routinely take home from their workplaces pads, pencils, paper clips and other office supplies for their personal use; many copy music CDs or illegally download music; students cheat on tests; many of us go to work late and leave early.

More than 70% of American drivers admit regularly driving faster than posted speed limits, and many use radar detectors to avoid detection. More than 60% of golfers admit cheating on their golf scores. And many others cheat without admitting it.

Our daughter took a day off work to let a plumber into her home between 8 and 10 a.m. By 10 no plumber, nor by 11. Nor by noon, when she went back to work. She called for an appointment on a different date when once again the plumber didn't show up. Most of us can relate to her experience.

In the property and casualty insurance business, where I spent my "first life," it is estimated 30 cents of every claim dollar are lost to "soft fraud," small time cheating by normally honest people.

One third of Americans say it is acceptable to exaggerate insurance claims to offset the deductibles. One of three says it's not wrong for a person to collect workers compensation even though able to return to work.

In some states there are three pending medical malpractice suits for every doctor. Certainly some claims are legitimate. But many of those claimants, maybe even a majority, are searching for "jackpot justice," a significant ethics problem in our country, not to mention a hefty cost factor that significantly increases the cost of medical care for all of us.

Does Anybody Care?

Newspaper reporters write stories that are untrue and create quotes that are untrue, and radio and television news reports express the personal bias of reporters, all in the interest of advancing a political agenda disguised as news.

Stock analysts promote a stock because of investment banking ties, not because it's a good investment.

Politicians give unbid contracts to relatives and political cronies and accept expensive gifts, free travel, elaborate golf outings, and other perks from constituents who hope for political favors. Illegal campaign contributions are nearly routine. And I firmly believe it is an ethics violation, if not out-and-out dishonesty, to vote on bills the politician hasn't read.

And the list goes on and on, from professional baseball players who use illegal bats to the United Nations. Every level of our society is involved—religious institutions, philanthropic organizations, labor unions, political parties, business organizations. No segment of civilization is exempt.

With ethics abuses so far reaching, what's the big deal about ethics? Does anybody really care?

Yes, your customers care. Successful salespeople who remain successful year after year are ethical people who do the right thing in their dealings with customers—always. Ethical people and ethical organizations tend to be successful over the long haul, and unethical people and organizations are likely to fail ultimately. Although at times it appears otherwise, "everybody" does not violate ethical standards.

A specific culture permeates every business organization. It's a philosophical framework that guides the actions of every person associated with an organization.

You can name companies for which you would not want to work. I know I can. Every person who works there says it's a lousy place to work. That's a philosophical framework—one you would not want to emulate. I know one company that takes apparent pride in calling itself a Burn 'Em and Churn 'Em Company. I know several people who work there, and make good money, but many of them tell me it isn't worth it. Interestingly, this company made the news recently in a corporate scandal. It was not a surprise.

Likewise, you and I can name companies that are good places to work. They have a great reputation of treating their people well. That's a philosophical framework.

And we can name companies where we don't want to do business. They have a reputation of taking advantage of customers whenever it might improve the profit picture. That's a philosophical framework—again, one we would not wish to copy.

And we can name companies where we enjoy doing business—because they give customers good service and good value. Always. That's a philosophical framework we should admire and emulate. That's the kind of a culture and philosophical framework super successful salespeople should build and in which they should operate.

Back in my corporate days, I regularly met with new employees. "Regardless of the circumstances, regardless of what the contract says, we always want you to do the right thing. Do you know what it means to do the right thing?" I asked.

After asking for definitions of "doing the right thing" hundreds of times, I've found most people have a pretty clear idea of how to define it. Should some unusual circumstance arise, and should a group be told they were expected to do the right thing, I've found in nearly every case there is complete agreement on what action would be most appropriate. They know how to do the right thing.

"If your actions are described on the front page of our local newspaper or *U.S.A Today* tomorrow, we would want most people to read the account and say, 'I think they did the right thing.' That's the kind of action we encourage and expect," I continued.

Recently I had an opportunity to ask the same question to a group of seventh graders. They too felt they had established a proper set of values that would enable them to "do the right thing" through high school, college and life.

These are the values the public expects of highly successful people. These are the values successful salespeople must demonstrate in all personal actions and business transactions.

I have in mind two salespeople. One is unmistakably a very successful person any salesperson would want to emulate. The other is, well, average. They operate in the same community with the same economy, the same competition, the same products and services, the same prices, the same everything. Both happen to be property and casualty insurance salespeople, but you could find parallels in most industries. I wish I could bring these two salespeople into a room with you right now so you could visit with them for awhile. After the visit, I would like to ask you to identify the salesperson who has achieved superior results and the one whose performance is average. Chances are you'd be wrong.

Salesperson No. 1 has a fantastic "sales personality." He has a winning smile; he's friendly; he's courteous. He meets many of the people-person characteristics we discussed earlier. He would be comfortable visiting with you, and you'd enjoy going to lunch or playing golf with him.

Salesperson No. 2 isn't unfriendly as such, but he comes through as being a little shy. He's not as outgoing as Salesperson No. 1. He's not especially good with small talk.

Which salesperson is the huge success? It's Salesperson No. 2. No. 2's success involves something much deeper, and much less obvious, than having a winning personality or being an excellent conversationalist. He always shoots straight. His word is solid gold. He does what he says he's going to do when he says he's going to do it. Always. He has integrity to the core.

Although it may not be obvious in an initial conversation, over time customers detect the differences between Salesperson No. 1 and Salesperson No. 2. If Salesperson No. 1 has to stretch the truth a bit to make a sale, he might be inclined to do so. And he may become just a little careless in following through on what he had promised. Or he might violate other principles of integrity, perhaps just slightly, if a sale depends on it, a quality that will soon become obvious to his customer base.

Salesperson No. 2 has a value system any of us would admire—an inner quality he would never compromise. His clients have learned over the long run they can trust him totally.

Now let's look at the sales records of Salesperson No. 1 and Salesperson No. 2. Remember, they operate in exactly the same market, with the same competition, the same economy, and even the same products and prices.

Salesperson No. 1's record of new sales isn't exactly shoddy. Typically each year he has an impressive record of new sales, some years up by 40% or more. Most sales people would walk through glass for such a sales increase. Salesperson No. 2 normally has more modest sales increases.

Over a period of years, however, Salesperson No. 1's commission income has remained relatively level while Salesperson No. 2's income has skyrocketed. Why? Over time Salesperson No. 1's customers have become disenchanted with his "service after the sale," which is critical in the property and casualty insurance business. As some customers become disenchanted or begin to question his integrity, they move to another agent.

Salesperson No. 2, on the other hand, has policy persistency of more than 95%. That is, he keeps more than 95% of his customers year after year. His customers stay with him because they are impressed with the value he provides. His customers, like customers in any industry, want to do business with a person they like and can trust totally.

There are salespeople like No. 1 and No. 2 in virtually every industry in America and in virtually every market in America. One succeeds overwhelmingly; the other just gets by. The successful salesperson has a genuine relationship with customers. He or she is truthful always; never lies or deceives; always delivers what's promised when it's promised; and has integrity to the core.

It's probably not a coincidence most highly successful salespeople I have observed through the years believe in God and are active in their places of worship. Although there are exceptions, most give credit to their parents and to their spiritual life for helping them establish their core values.

Customers like to do business with salespeople who possess praiseworthy value systems. But they don't advertise it, boast or brag about it. Customers will know soon enough about the ethics, trustworthiness, character and integrity of any salesperson without being told.

High ethical standards are essential qualities that help you *Super-Size Your Sales*.

LEAVE A MESSAGE AT THE TONE

Handling phone calls is a delicate balance between having a phone at your ear continuously for 16 hours a day and using phone mail to such an extreme customer relationships are impaired. Successful sales people have generally learned how to achieve an appropriate balance.

It's a fact customers are generally unhappy with phone mail. Audiences to whom I speak across the country tell me consistently this is the single most disturbing aspect of dealing with most American businesses. "I can't talk to a human being," customers complain. "I'm convinced no human actually works there."

By the time callers listen to and select the menu option most appropriate, they're too frustrated to leave a message, or forget why they called, when they hear, "Please leave a message at the tone."

Obviously, no salesperson (or anyone else for that matter) can be—or should be—available by phone 24/7. Yet great salespeople have learned how to enhance customer relationships, maintain close customer contact, and assure customers receive the overwhelming service they have a right to expect.

When customer service reps are available to help with service after the sale, the outstanding salesperson introduces that person during the sales process and provides contact information to the customer: "When I'm not available, Judy is here to help you. Please don't hesitate to call her."

When customer service reps are not available, many successful salespeople set a telephone expectation standard during the sales presentation. One successful insurance agent says during the sales presentation, "Our company gives excellent service. But, as you can imagine, I can't always be immediately available by phone. But normally I'll get back to you within an hour and always the same business day." Now the customer knows what to anticipate. In view of most phone experiences with most businesses, an approach like this will not cause many customers to feel the phone service the salesperson has offered is inferior. Most buyers regularly call "big outfits" that have a near-endless supply of human resources and experience a maddening tangle of phone messages.

Here's another example of outstanding customer service provided by America's top salespeople: They turn over their business cards and *write* their home numbers and cell numbers on the back and say, "This will assure you that you'll always be able to reach me when you need service of any kind." Customers are always impressed with this *special* service of having a private number.

Salespeople who make their personal numbers available to clients claim nearly every customer respects their personal time. There are few hassles at night and over weekends. My personal experience as CEO of a major company was similar. My home number was available to employees, agents, and even policyholders and claimants. We always had a listed number. There was only one instance throughout my career in which I was harassed by an irate claimant.

Successful businesses keep their phone mail greetings as simple as possible. Callers are universally irritated when they have to go through a series of menu items that would challenge a nuclear scientist. Top salespeople provide an easy way for callers to leave their names and numbers without enduring a near-endless array of phone mail options. My recommendation is there should never be more than one simple message before a human answers. But doesn't this increase overhead costs? Perhaps—a little. But it costs a lot more to win back a good customer who has been offended by an irritating phone mail game.

As a business grows, most sales people will work out a system to give clients immediate phone contact with a human. Client calls should not become a burden; spending every evening on the phone isn't fair to the salesperson's family. Any super-human will eventually burn out with 80-hour work weeks; and everybody deserves a vacation now and then. With further growth in sales and staffing, a member of the staff should be assigned to phone service on a rotating basis evenings and weekends. Another solution proven effective by many successful salespeople is to use a professional answering service or a part-timer who works at home, paid on a per-call basis, to whom calls can be rolled when the salesperson is not available.

I'm reminded of an insurance agency principal who dropped by his agency at 11 o'clock Saturday evening to pick up a personal item. While in his office the phone rang and he answered it. "Paul," the caller said as he identified himself, "I sold the old '98 Buick and bought a new Cadillac. Would you make the change in my insurance policy for me?" Paul took the required information and told his client his policy would be endorsed promptly.

As he left the office, Paul thought, "My client didn't seem a bit surprised I was in my office and answered the phone at 11 p.m. Saturday. He expected me to be here."

This is typical of American consumers today. They expect service 24/7. And for good reason. A lot is going on in the American economy during evenings and weekends. For instance, a large automobile dealer says 70% of new cars are sold on Friday nights, Saturdays and Sundays, a time when most of us are not open for business.

America's top salespeople have Super-Sized their sales by developing a system that provides the type of service American consumers are screaming for: *instant* service; *personal* attention; right *now*; when it's convenient for you, the buyer; not necessarily when it's convenient for me, the salesperson. And they use the telephone as a tool to enhance the quality of service they render to their clients.

THE ELECTRONIC YELLOW PAGES

"What's the value of a salesperson," someone asked me not long ago, "when that's such an old fashioned way of doing business? Everybody today does business on the Internet."

Yes, the Internet is a fact of life and, with the vast availability of information on nearly any topic, it has changed the way many personal and business decisions are made. The Internet is the new Electronic Yellow Pages. Every business—every sales person—must use the Internet to advantage just as we use (or once used) the Yellow Pages.

In my own business, I can't say how many sales result from my Web site. I doubt many sales result from the site alone. But I can say virtually everyone who contacts me has read my Web site. Therefore, it's clear my Web site is a critical dimension of my sales effort.

Today's shoppers are better informed, regardless of the type of product or service offered. They do their homework, thanks to the Internet. The Internet is a place to do research; it's a sales brochure; it's a catalog. But the Internet alone is not a very good cash register unless you're selling a commodity—which means every product is the same, the service is the same, the sales person adds no value, and the only buyer motivation is price.

We've already discussed the importance of not permitting your product or service to become a commodity. Another salesperson or another form of marketing will always be able to sell cheaper. Your Web site must be designed to bring attention to the value you provide and the benefits you offer.

Direct marketing is not new. Richard Warren Sears and Alvah Curtis Roebuck tried it in 1888 with the first Sears-Roebuck catalog, a mailer devoted to watches and jewelry. But even then, Sears and Roebuck tried to avoid the "commodity" effect by promising, "We warrant every American watch sold by us, with fair usage, an accurate time keeper for six years—during which time, under our written guarantee, we are compelled to keep it in perfect order free of charge."

The catalog sales trend continued to expand, fueled by the westward expansion of the railroads, by Rural Free Delivery in 1896, and by special postal rates of one cent per pound for "aids in the dissemination of knowledge."

As Sears' direct mail sales concept expanded, its customer service efforts expanded as well. The 1903 catalog included the commitment "Your money back if you are not satisfied" and informed the public they employed translators who can "read and write all languages." Even then, personal relationships were emphasized.

To encourage repeat customers, a "customer profit sharing" program was introduced giving the customer a certificate for every dollar spent which could be accumulated and redeemed for specific items.

The 1905 catalog included wallpaper samples and swatches of materials used in clothing. As the catalog sales concept expanded, there were continuing efforts to add value to the transaction.

Although Sears still distributes many specialty catalogs for tools, auto accessories, home improvements, etc., the general catalog was eliminated in 1993. Now Sears features on-line sites through its Shop at Home concept. In other words, for the most part the catalog is now electronic. Now the store's Web site boasts, "Buy online, then go to the store and get your item within five minutes."

One K-Mart store (K-Mart and Sears are owned by the same holding company) is being converted to a pickup-only site for Internet orders.

The evolution of the Sears catalog parallels in many ways the development of modern day sales, with increasing emphasis on adding value to the transaction.

Web marketing certainly has several distinct values. Buyers want to be informed buyers. They want to be smart enough to know if the salesperson is shooting straight with them. For instance, what do people hate most about buying a car? Haggling. The Web helps level the haggling field. They get information on sticker prices and dealers' invoice prices, then go to the dealer as an educated buyer.

Many buyers prefer independent sites not sponsored by a manufacturer. They want to make sure the information they're getting is valid.

One study showed people who shopped on the Web before buying a car fared a little better on price when they visited the dealer. Other studies are less conclusive.

The Electronic Yellow Pages

Internet marketers often do a better job of cross selling than many sales people. Note Amazon.com's success with its reminder, "People who buy this book are also buying this one." This technique is one more sales people should be emulating.

Use your Web site as an adjunct to your sales efforts. The Internet should complement your normal sales program, not replace it.

Recognize the limitations of the Web. One expert maintains no search engine indexes more than 16% of the total pages available. The pages number into the hundreds of millions.

For several years a number of grocery stores tried Web sales but found it costs too much to pick, pack and deliver the average grocery order. Often customers were not at home when the order arrived. A charge for delivery was rejected by most buyers. For the most part the concept failed. Now the concept has transitioned to an easy on-line system to order groceries the consumer can pick up, prepacked, at a set time.

An insurance company that had operated through local independent agents tried an intensive Web marketing experiment but discontinued it after a several million dollar investment. "Customers want a trusted adviser to guide them through the insurance transaction," the company's president said, "from buying appropriate protection to servicing their business." He went on to say, "People want to shop over the Net but not necessarily buy."

Experiments like these made it clear the Internet must complement normal sales efforts, not replace them.

Many of today's Internet sales come from folks who have in the past been comfortable with other forms of direct marketing, such as phone or direct mail. They are comfortable buying a product without touching it or talking to people. (In my former field of property and casualty insurance, these customers comprise about 10% to 12% of the market.)

For the most part, the Internet may help the buyer find someone to talk to, but they still *want* someone to talk to. Shoppers still like to take their kids to the mall to sit on Santa's lap. They still like to be with people. (Solitary confinement is still the most cruel form of human punishment. People can't stand to be alone for any length of time.)

One study found shoppers are three times more likely to buy if they speak with a sales person. And they are more likely to dial a local number than an 800 number.

Recognizing the role the Internet plays in arranging travel, a travel agents' trade association ran an ad series, "Without a travel agent, you're on your own." I can tell you from personal experience, the last thing a traveler wants is to be "on your own." Perhaps Internet-arranged travel makes more sense for the leisure traveler who has a flexible schedule. But when a business traveler's schedule changes—"I've got to be there by noon tomorrow instead of by 4 p.m."—it's a frustrating feeling trying to unravel the mess.

Buyers not only want to do business with people, they want to do business with "people like me." One direct-response insurance company placed a second call center in Georgia. They found people in the South like to do business with Southerners.

A Texas banker, on a business trip to London, called for a car to transport him to the airport. A woman with a British accent answered the phone. As soon as she heard the man's voice, she switched to a Texas drawl. "Who are you?" the man asked. It was a call center in Bangalore. The woman had learned to match a Texas accent from having watched *Walker, Texas Ranger* on TV.

If you don't already have a Web site, develop one. Do

it right, with attractive graphics and well written copy. Briefly point out the benefits you provide to customers—always from the customer's perspective, not your own. This is your sales brochure. It must be professional.

Over time, learn to use Facebook, Twitter, LinkedIn, and other forms of social media.

Set up Google and Twitter alerts to see what others might be saying about you and your company. It's nice to hear good things, but it's even more critical to hear the bad things, for you need to know what you might be doing wrong and should correct.

Consider writing a blog. If you choose to have one, it must be well written and must be current. If you're not a good writer or don't have time to update it two or three times a week, find someone to write it for you. Content must be about helping customers, not blatant, in-your-face selling.

These forms of "electronic yellow pages" are communication tools. They give prominence to your name and will bring people to you. Then it's a matter of value—value that's added by a professional sales person.

ASK

A friend has been a salesperson, and a very successful one, all his adult life. He is well known and well liked. He's involved in a number of social groups in his church and his community. Everyone knows the type of business he's in and has respect for his knowledge, ethics and reputation in general.

After a several year relationship, one of his friends made a purchase of a product elsewhere. My sales friend said, "You know, I sell the same type of product, and I could have gotten you a good deal and would have provided excellent service as well."

"Yes, I know," his friend responded. "But I've known you more than 15 years and you've never suggested I buy from you. I thought you didn't want my business."

My sales friend had been fearful of taking advantage of personal relationships. He thought invitations to buy might be viewed as pressure or harassment when, in fact, he would have been doing his friends a favor.

Every great salesperson must find a comfortable way of saying, "I would appreciate the opportunity to do business with you. I will always give you great value." This applies to friends and family as well.

Always complete the sales process by asking for the business: "You will find that our product (or service) will serve you well, and we would appreciate the opportunity to do business with you."

And when you get the business, always say "thanks" and express your appreciation once again, followed by a handwritten personal note in a hand addressed and stamped envelope.

Every customer should be treated like a good friend or family member. So it follows friends and family should be treated as customers. Everyone who knows you is assured of getting great value from you. Everyone who knows you knows you are an expert in your field. Everyone who knows you knows you'll treat them fairly. You're the kind of salesperson everyone wants to do business with, so why keep it a secret? Why not give them an opportunity to do business with you?

This means you must ask for the business. It's a basic rule of salesmanship too often overlooked.

PROGRAMMED TO WIN

On several occasions in my former company we found one salesperson in one sales territory was consistently successful, regardless of conditions. Another salesperson in another sales territory was consistently unsuccessful—because he had a bad territory, the unemployment rate was higher in that particular region, the clientele in that territory were especially cost conscious, or some other creative reason.

So we would switch the territories, and in a few months the successful salesperson was once again consistently successful and the unsuccessful salesperson was consistently unsuccessful.

Why? Because one salesperson was programmed to win and the other was programmed to fail.

How does one become programmed to win? By building a positive sales environment in which to work and by avoiding the negative influences all around us that program us to fail.

We often become programmed to fail because we haven't learned to absorb the normal, everyday problems that are an integral part of life. Everybody has problems. There are financial problems, marital problems, kid problems, health problems, employer problems. You name it, over the course of a career, most of us will encounter several of these problems.

Then we top it off by watching the 11 o'clock news to hear about another murder, two rapes, a house fire killing two children, a severe automobile accident killing one and seriously injuring two, a major local employer terminating 300 employees in a cost reduction move, and the weatherman is forecasting crummy weather again tomorrow.

I don't mean to minimize the personal problems we face, but life would be boring without them. If we didn't have any problems we would have to create some. The golf course designers are doing a pretty good job of it. They are coming up with many ways to make a person feel miserable after a round of golf: water everyplace; roughs so tall anyone under 5-9 will get lost; and greens on those little islands.

People aren't just running marathons, it's marathons at the Arctic Circle, up 3,700 steps at the Great Wall of China, or 100 mile mega-marathons run over a 24 hour period. It's inherent in the human makeup to create obstacles if there aren't any.

The human being is meant to be challenged. The human mind and body are meant to be stretched. We need "sand traps" and "water hazards" in our lives.

I'm convinced the news media and politicians on both sides of the political aisle have a mission statement intended to help every person become programmed to fail.

On July 10, 1821, the United States purchased the province of East Florida from Spain for $5 million, over the objection of many members of Congress. One Congressman strenuously opposed the purchase, saying Florida was nothing but swamps, insects and reptiles. He insisted no one would ever settle in Florida—"No sir. No man would immigrate into Florida—no, not from hell itself." This began a long tradition of politicians lying to the American people.

In 1968 it was predicted hundreds of millions of people will starve because of the population explosion. In 1972 the world's economy would fail because we were running out of oil, gas, silver, tin, uranium, aluminum, copper, lead and zinc. In 1977 we were warned all oil reserves in the entire world would be used up by the end of the next decade. Acid rain in 1986 was blamed for damaging a quarter of Europe's trees. Also in 1986 the Chernobyl nuclear reactor was said to threaten the death of millions of people. In 1996 some 500,000 people faced death because of BSE, a brain disease transmitted by infected beef. In 2000 the Y2K problem would cause planes to fall from the air and bring the world's economy to its knees. Other crises include acid rain, bird flu, death by fluoride, SARS, toxic PVC and poisonous breast implants, to name just a few.

As this is being written, the World Health Organization has confirmed 14,000 deaths in the world from H1N1, or swine flu, which was predicted to be so devastating. That's a tragic number, but it pales in comparison to the 500,000 people who lose their lives each year from regular old seasonal flu.

A Japanese professor said we humans are risking extinction because heels are getting rounder and jaws are getting smaller. We will lose our ability to stand up or eat—in just one million years. I must make a note on my calendar.

A more recent concern is global warming which some say will ultimately cause the ice cap to melt and ocean levels to rise, submerging many coastal cities. Global warming has been blamed for hurricanes, tornadoes, malaria, the Minneapolis bridge collapse, teenage drinking, terrorism, too much snow, too little snow, Atlantic ocean less salty, Atlantic ocean more salty, Earth slowing down, Earth speeding up, bigger fish, smaller fish, better beer, worse beer, and even the irritability of mice.

There have been warming trends, and cooling trends, in this world over the past 3,000 years. There have been five extended periods when the atmosphere was warmer than it is today. Today's temperatures remain below the 3,000 year average.

The hottest year on record was 1934, 2/100s of one degree Celsius warmer than the second warmest year 1998. Six of the hottest years on record were in the 1930s and 1940s. At one time, Greenland, now 85% covered by ice, was green.

In the early 1970s scientists were concerned about global cooling. They predicted the next ice age. They said the world's population would starve because we would be unable to grow crops on the ice cap. Global cooling was featured on the cover of *Time* magazine on June 24, 1974.

Today the polar bear population is increasing, not declining as widely reported. While some glaciers are melting, others are growing.

Yes, there will be warming trends and cooling trends, just as there have been over the past 3000 years. Keep in mind weather forecasters have trouble predicting the weather tomorrow afternoon, not to mention a hundred years from now.

This is typical of the crises we have faced through the years. Of course, most of those crises never occurred and have long been forgotten. And if we don't rush in with solutions that make the matter worse, these current day crises will be forgotten as well.

Lenin, a Russian politician and revolutionary (1870-1924) said, "A lie told often enough becomes the truth." Lenin's tactics are widely in use today.

Avoid the many "programmed to fail" influences all around us. Concentrate on the "programmed to win" influences that are everywhere if we look for them.

First, **stop complaining**. Public speaker Cavett Robert once said 80% of the people don't care about your problems; the other 20% are glad you've got them. Although obviously an exaggeration in the interest of humor, it's probably closer to the truth than we would like to think. Most people are interested only in themselves and their own families.

Recognize the world is made up of hills and valleys. Falling down periodically is a part of life. We would not have learned to walk had we not fallen down time and again.

Learn to love the problems that are inherent in any worthwhile activity. Love the challenges of sales and business. These are simply hurdles that keep life interesting, free of boredom, and help us perform up to our potential. That's why a sports team often performs best when it faces its toughest competitor of the season and why it lets down and often loses when it believes its opponent will be a pushover.

Successful salespeople know if it were easy, everybody would be doing it. And we think we have competition now. If it were easy, the job simply wouldn't provide the challenge and stimulation most of us require.

When the economy is flat and sales are tougher than normal, successful people recognize the competitors are having as tough a time as they are. And during these "down" periods, competitors become depressed and tend not to work as hard as normal. Great salespeople know this is the time to make calls on new customers who have had a business relationship with a competitor.

Successful salespeople recognize the role a positive attitude plays. There's a classic business school parable about two shoe salesmen who were assigned to a remote African community. The first wired his home office, "Am returning immediately. No one here wears shoes." The other wired, "Send a steamer load of shoes immediately. No one here wears shoes."

Learn to love what you do. "If you hate to go to work tomorrow, don't go," I often told the employees of my former company. "Find something you love. Nobody has ever been successful unless they truly loved what they do." Overwhelmingly successful people like McDonald's Ray Kroc, Sam Walton of Walmart and Microsoft's Bill Gates all loved their work. And it showed with unbelievable results.

Debbie Fields Rose is the person behind Mrs. Fields Cookies. She loved to make cookies, and "I still love sharing them," she says. "I didn't have any credentials. I didn't have a business degree, a college degree or any business experience other than working since I was 13 in retail… Other than that, I made great cookies….Everybody was convinced I was never going to make anything of myself…I found so much discouragement it made me feisty and made me want to go out and prove to myself, if for no other reason, that I could do it."

She moved to open-air stores, so prospective customers could smell the aroma of freshly baked cookies as they strolled the shopping malls.

"We're in the business of having fun," she says. New employees are told on the first day on the job they are expected to ensure customers always leave with smiles on their faces. Her success has shown having fun pays off. Over the years, however, the company grew too rapidly and became too diversified. They got away from their core business; they took their eyes off the ball and the company sold in 1993.

One of the nation's largest and most successful automobile dealers was asked in a magazine interview about the secret of the agency's success. "We make buying an automobile fun," the dealer answered.

Surveys have shown fast-food restaurants are not satisfying customers' needs for friendly service. NFO World Group says one-third of fast-food customers are dissatisfied with their dining experience. They want competent, friendly service—a smile with their meals.

In my former job as a CEO of a major company, there were days when there was an avalanche of problems from every direction—from regulators, investors, the sales force, claimants. Most communications were negative. Seldom did anyone call to say, "This is a wonderful insurance company that's fun to do business with." Instead, most callers said, "Here's my problem. Now what are you going to do about it?" At times the weight of those problems was enormous. It would have been easy to get the impression my company was not a very good one.

It takes a conscious effort to remember the majority of our customers were happy with our products and service and any service breakdown was an exception. And I reminded myself to have confidence in our outstanding staff to put a fix in place to avoid the exception in the future.

Unless there is a conscious effort to remain positive, it's easy to create mental self doubt. Like most successful salespeople, I learned how to deal with the body slams of life. It's not that successful people are born with some unique smiley-face gene permitting them to remain optimistic, positive, upbeat and to have fun. I'm convinced it's possible to *learn* to laugh and see the lighter side of the world around us. It just takes concentration and practice. When an especially maddening experience is about to occur, I tell myself, "*Nothing* can make me mad. I'm going to find the humor in this." When I approach the situation in this manner, I find it works nearly without exception.

It will work for you too. Anybody with an intense desire and commitment to become positive can develop a habit of being upbeat and optimistic in about 30 days. Here are my simple rules of overcoming, and preventing, a bad day:

Act positive. Act like today is a great day. When you act like it's a terrific day, it isn't long until you don't have to act. The day really *is* a great day.

It's not hard to act once you recognize there's value in everything that happens. Although elusive at times, when we look back, the value becomes apparent in the event that once seemed so devastating. Have faith in God's plan for each of us.

The media has a dramatic influence on each of us, in a relatively few minutes each day we read newspapers or watch TV news. Just think of the positive influence we can have on our own minds by planting positive thoughts throughout the day.

Read something inspirational every day. All of us need regular reinforcement and encouragement. Too often we don't get it—and you can be nearly certain the more successful you are, and the higher you rise in your organization, the less reinforcement and encouragement you will receive. Therefore, you have to provide it yourself—by reading inspirational materials. This is still a part of my daily routine.

A friend, Ralph Walls, wrote a book entitled *Breakfast With God* (Peppertree Press – 2009). Ralph's inspirational time is the first thing in the morning before getting involved with the day's activities. My inspiration time is just before bedtime. I like to "clean my pockets" of all the junk that has accumulated during the day, setting the framework for a good night's sleep. This inspiration time is my "self cleaning oven" which gets rid of all the gunk that tends to stick to my mind. Early or late, it doesn't matter. The choice is yours.

I'm a fan of the writings of Dr. Norman Vincent Peale, author of the classic *The Power of Positive Thinking*. I read it and re-read it, along with other Peale books. Whatever modest success I've achieved in the business world must be attributed to these books more than any other single factor.

Another favorite is a little magazine from the Peale Foundation for Christian Living entitled *Positive Thinking*. *Guideposts* magazine is also a worthwhile read.

On the mandatory reading list is my book, *What Do You Do When You're Having a Bad Day?* (Peppertree Press – 2008). Everybody has bad days now and then, and this book will help you learn to deal with them. Please excuse this blatant commercial message.

And don't forget the Bible. Whatever problem you may be encountering, there's a verse in the Bible that speaks to it.

Get some rest. Problems, I have found, are smaller and can be digested more easily when I am rested. When I arrive home at 1:00 a.m. after a late flight and the starting gun goes off at 5:00 a.m., the problems emerging during the day are bigger. After a good night's sleep, the problem that seemed so weighty the day before doesn't seem so big. The solution is more readily apparent.

Cut out the TV time and whenever possible go to bed early.

Build a positive, capable team. None of us, not even Superman, can carry every burden alone. Every successful person needs the support of a competent team. With a great team, any problem becomes manageable.

Have fun. The outstanding people on our team kept the environment positive and fun. We worked hard and we laughed hard. We learned we must not take ourselves too seriously. The words *humor* and *humility* are rooted in the same Greek word.

Having fun on the job doesn't involve a cast of stand-up comedians who try to keep everyone on staff entertained. It's not telling jokes as such, certainly not off-color jokes. Rather, it involves building a team of compatible people who have a sense of humor, who are fun to be with, who show kindness and respect for one another, and who have learned to make every business transaction a pleasant experience. People want to be a part of a winning team. They want to contribute to a worthwhile mission—a mission everyone shares and believes in. But they want to pursue the mission in a pleasant working environment.

A fun, pleasant environment does not impede productivity. Work effort actually increases in an enjoyable atmosphere.

Cape Air/Nantucket Airlines has a slogan I love—MOCHA HAGoTDI—Make Our Customers Happy and Have A Good Time Doing It. Cape Air/Nantucket is saying, "It's okay to have fun on the job as long as our customers are happy. And our customers are more likely to be happy when you are having fun." MOCHA HAGoTDI is a brilliant mantra, one we should all emulate.

Southwest Airlines similarly encourages its employees to have fun on the job. When I fly Southwest, the positive attitudes and friendly spirit of Southwest employees are contagious. When I arrive at my destination, I find I'm not as tired as I am following most flights and I feel more energetic and enthusiastic as I pursue my work agenda for the day. All of us feel better when we're around pleasant, enthusiastic, friendly people.

Laughter heals. Laughter produces endorphins which have been proven to help cure many diseases, including cancer. If laughter can have such a positive effect on curing illnesses, think of its influence on your ability to deal with the challenges that are a part of life and to help you remain positive and upbeat, no matter what hurdles you face.

When you become more positive and visualize success, you'll automatically become more successful. Darrell Burnett in his book *Youth Sports and Self Esteem—A Guide for Parents* tells of an experiment with three groups of people shooting basketball free throws. Group A practiced every day; Group B was told *not* to practice; and Group C was told not to touch the ball but visualize shooting free shots ten minutes a day. Group A improved 25%; Group B didn't improve at all; and Group C improved 23% even though they didn't touch the ball.

Emery University in Georgia has conducted studies along the same line. They found the same chemicals were activated in the brain for a group that jogged in place and one that only *visualized* jogging in place.

In your business too, visualizing success creates certain brain activity that is more likely to bring about success. The more clearly you see it, the more likely it is to happen.

Unhappy people seldom treat customers the way the customers have a right to be treated. A recent survey found 72% of the some 140 million gainfully employed people in this country don't like their jobs and/or their bosses. Some 50% have already checked out mentally in that they are either actively looking for another job now or would take another job should one be offered. It's easy to understand why service levels in America have deteriorated. And it's easy to understand why so many people are not successful in their life's work.

Look at your own buying patterns. Chances are you have some reluctance to do repeat business with people who have sour attitudes. Price doesn't matter. The quality of the product doesn't matter. You seek out sales people who are pleasant to deal with.

Everybody wants to do business with people who are cheerful, positive, enthusiastic, and up-beat. When there are positive people working in a positive environment, there is electricity in the air. It's fun to work in an environment like this. When people are having fun, success is more likely. A person who hates to go to work tomorrow will not be successful. Also, you'll feel better; you'll take greater pride in being a professional sales person; you'll enjoy life more; and you'll attract more potential customers to you.

The principles we've discussed in this book can be put to work by anyone with an intense desire and a strong commitment to succeed. You can rise above the rank and file. You can be overwhelmingly successful. This formula to *Super-Size Your Sales* works like magic—every time.

OTHER BOOKS BY ROBERT L. BAILEY

The New Leader - **Peppertree Press**
   Promotions are one of life's most challenging times, even ahead of death of a family member, divorce, moving and managing teenage children. This book will help you approach the job with confidence, encourage your employees to buy-in to your organization's mission, and guide you to become a truly effective leader. You'll learn what you should do on your first few days and weeks on the job; the critically important principle that drives all effective leadership; why most leaders fail; and how to keep employees motivated.

What Do You Do When You're Having A Bad Day? - **Peppertree Press**
   Having a great day every day is a learned skill, one that can be developed by anyone. Personal problems and

annoyances need not drag you down. Learn how to unlock a power so strong even many physical illnesses can be cured; establish a positive point of view in 20 to 30 days; solve problems while you sleep; find the joy in your work; bring quiet and order to your life; solve your financial problems; and use humor to lessen tensions and break the monotony of life.

Plain Talk About Leadership – Franklin University Press

This is about leadership in the real world. You will learn how to become a more effective leader, build a positive corporate culture, create a productive work environment, build a team of first-rate people, improve customer service and customer relationships, control expenses, and keep staffing at the proper level.

To schedule the author for speaking engagements, or to purchase books in quantity, visit:

www.bobbaileyspeaker.com
or contact him at bobbailey1@comcast.net
or 941-358-5260.

THE AUTHOR

Bob Bailey often refers to himself as "self unemployed" since his retirement from corporate life in 2000. But he is far from unemployed.

He is the retired CEO, President and Chairman of the State Auto Insurance Companies, is the author of the books *What Do You Do When You're Having a Bad Day?* (Peppertree Press – 2008); *The New Leader* (Peppertree Press – 2008); P*lain Talk About Leadership* (Franklin University Press – 2002) and is a columnist for *Rough Notes* magazine. He has a rather intense schedule as a professional public speaker helping people like you become more successful. These activities produce a work schedule that would challenge most people half his age.

Under his leadership of the State Auto Insurance Companies since 1983, the company became one of the top performing property and casualty insurance companies in the United States. Several companies were added to the State Auto Group. The company entered 13 additional states and became publicly owned in 1991 with the formation of State Auto Financial Corporation.

Since the Financial Corporation's first full year as a public corporation through his retirement, compound average annual growth rates were: revenues 14%; earnings per share 23%; equity 14%; assets 17%; and book value per share 16%. From 1991 through 1997, State Auto stock was the 85th best performer on the NASDAQ exchange.

Under his leadership, sales rose from $214 million to more than $1 billion, net worth increased from $129 million to nearly $1 billion, and service levels were improved dramatically under what he calls an "overwhelming service" objective. At the same time employee morale rose to the highest level ever, thanks to a strong focus on communication, recognition and motivation. The accomplishments of the Companies have been noted in publications by Tom Peters, co-author of the best selling books on business management, *In Search of Excellence, A Passion for Excellence*, and others.

Bob entered the insurance business in 1958 with the Western Casualty and Surety Company of Fort Scott, Kansas (now a part of the Liberty Group)—near the farm where he was raised and where he attended a one-room country school. He is quick to point out that for six of the eight years of elementary school he was the top student in class. After a few seconds hesitation, he adds, "I was also the bottom student in class—I was the only one. By the time I made it to the eighth grade, I'd been through it seven times."

He is a graduate of Pittsburg (Kansas) State University following two years at Fort Scott (Kansas) Community College, where he was named its outstanding alumnus in 2001. In 2007 he received the Meritorious Achievement Award from Pittsburg State, the highest honor Pitt State bestows on its alumni. In 2000 the Professional Insurance Agents Association named him the Insurance Industry Person of the Year. Franklin University, where he served as chairman and a board member for many years, awarded him an honorary doctorate degree in 2006.

In response to a number of honors he has received through the years, he says, "I think I've got this figured out. They do this alphabetically. It took them 50 years to get to the Bs. If your name is Smith or Wilson, you don't have a chance."

He holds the Chartered Property and Casualty Underwriter (CPCU) designation, the equivalent of CPA in accounting, and is an Associate in Risk Management.

As one might expect for a person with his executive talent, he has served on, and has been chairman of, a long list of community and industry boards. He is a member of the National Speakers Association and the Sarasota Baptist Church.

Bob Bailey is a dynamic person with a great sense of humor. He has a valuable, feet-on-the-ground real-world message that can help you *Super-Size Your Sales*—starting today.

Julie Ann Howell
Peppertree Press

www.ingramcontent.com/pod-product-compliance
Lightning Source LLC
Chambersburg PA
CBHW031924240526
45464CB00022B/769